# THE FILM NOVELIST

# THE FILM
# NOVELIST

Writing a Screenplay and Short Novel in
15 Weeks

## Dennis J. Packard

continuum

Continuum International Publishing Group
80 Maiden Lane, New York, NY 10038
The Tower Building, 11 York Road, London SE1 7NX

www.continuumbooks.com

Library of Congress Cataloging-in-Publication Data
Packard, Dennis J.
The film novelist: writing a screenplay and short novel in 15 weeks / Dennis J.
Packard.
p. cm.
Includes bibliographical references and index.
ISBN 978-1-4411-0317-8 (pbk. : alk. paper)    1. Motion picture authorship.
2. Film adaptations – Authorship.    3. Fiction – Authorship. I. Title.
PN1996.P225 2011
808.2'3—dc22
                                        2011012186

ISBN: 978-1-4411-0317-8 (paperback)



Typeset by Newgen Imaging Systems Pvt Ltd, Chennai, India
Printed and bound in the United States of America

# CONTENTS

# Acknowledgments

*Anton Chekhov's The Duel.* Directed by Dover Koshashvili. Duel Productions, 2010.

*Antwone Fisher.* Directed by Denzel Washington. Fox Searchlight Pictures, 2002.

*As Good as it Gets.* Directed by James L. Brooks. TriStar Pictures and Gracie Films, 1997.

*Barry Lyndon.* Directed by Stanley Kubrick. Peregrine, Hawk Films, and Warner Bros. Pictures, 1975.

*Bicycle Thieves.* Directed by Vittorio De Sica. ENIC, l948.

*Cache.* Directed by Michael Haneke. Les Films du Losange and Wega Film, 2005.

*The Dark Knight.* Directed by Christopher Nolan. Warner Bros. Pictures, 2008.

*Driving Miss Daisy.* Directed by Bruce Beresford. The Zanuck Company, 1989.

*Forrest Gump.* Directed by Robert Zemeckis. Paramount Pictures, 1994.

*Harry Potter and the Order of the Phoenix.* Directed by David Yates. Warner Bros. Pictures, 2007.

*It's a Wonderful Life.* Directed by Frank Capra. Liberty Films (II), 1947.

*Jaws.* Directed by Steven Spielberg. Universal Pictures, 1975.

*The Magnificent Ambersons.* Directed by Orson Welles. Mercury Productions and RKO Radio Pictures, 1942.

*The Maltese Falcon.* Directed by John Huston. Warner Bros. Pictures, 1941.

*Minority Report.* Directed by Steven Spielberg. Twentieth Century Fox Film Corporation, 2002.

*Misfits.* Directed by John Huston. Seven Arts Productions, 1961.

*Monsters, Inc.* Directed by Pete Docter. Pixar Animation Studios and Walt Disney Pictures, 2001.

*My Father's Glory.* Directed by Yves Robert. Gaumont, 1991.

*Of Mice and Men.* Directed by Lewis Milestone. United Artists, 1939.

*On the Waterfront.* Directed by Elia Kazan. Columbia Pictures, 1954.

Palzoo Celebrity Database. "Jean Renoir." Accessed February 18, 2011. http://www.palzoo.net/Jean-Renoir.

*Rocky.* Directed by John G. Avildsen. Chartoff-Winkler Productions and United Artists, 1976.

*Rules of the Game.* Directed by Jean Renoir. Nouvelles Éditions de Films, 1939

*The Shawshank Redemption.* Directed by Frank Darabont. Castle Rock Entertainment, 1994.

Sakamoto, Mamoru. "Portrait," on Yoshi Oida's official website, accessed February 18, 2011, www.yoshioida.com/portrait.

*Sounder.* Directed by Martin Ritt. Radnitz/Mattel Productions and Twentieth Century Fox Film Corporation, 1973.

*To Kill a Mockingbird.* Directed by Robert Mulligan. Universal International Pictures (UI), 1962.

*Tootsie.* Directed by Sydney Pollack. Columbia Pictures, 1982.

*The White Ribbon.* Directed by Michael Haneke. X-Filme Creative Pool, Wega Film, Les Films du Losagne, and Lucky Red, 2009.

The following images were taken from Wikimedia Commons and are public domain: Aristotle, Jane Austen, Andre Bazin, Miguel de Cervantes, Anton Chekhov, Jacques Derrida, Carl Dreyer, Sergei Eisenstein, William Faulkner, Giovanni Andrea de Ferrari's *Joseph's Coat Brought to Jacob*, Gustave Flaubert, D. W. Griffith, Dashiell Hammett, Michael Haneke, Martin Heidegger, John Huston, J. P. Jacobsen, James Joyce, Charles Sanders Peirce, Bertrand Russell, Jean-Paul Sartre, Constantin Stanislavski, John Steinbeck, Alfred North Whitehead, Tobias Wolff, Virginia Woolf.

I appreciate the generous help I have received on this book from Charles Cranney, Dean Duncan, Judy Garvin, Sibyl Johnston, Bruce Jorgensen, Darl Larsen, Robert Nelson, Rebecca McFadden Packard, Seth Packard, Jay Packard, Raymond Robinson, Eric Samuelsen,

Lyman Dayton, Linda Adams and Mel Thorne and their editing students, and my editors, Madeleine Dresden and Sandra Packard, my wife. My thoughts about writing and filming have been deeply influenced by David Warner, with whom I have collaborated for many years.

# Introduction

In 1930 Dashiell Hammett published *The Maltese Falcon,* the first film novel. *The Maltese Falcon* was filmed the very next year, again five years later, and then finally, through a series of fortuitous events, definitively in 1941 by John Huston. Huston had been writing scripts at Warner Brothers for nine years when Jack Warner gave him the chance to direct a film. According to Huston's co-writer, after the interview with Warner, Huston "tossed *The Maltese Falcon* on his desk, took a stance, pointed a finger at the book, and said, 'Kid, Warner said if I can get a good screenplay out of this Dash Hammett thing, he'll let me direct it.'"[1] Huston's co-writer thought that rescripting the novel was a dumb idea because the book had already been filmed twice.

The Maltese Falcon, 1941

**John Huston**

After watching the former two films, Huston decided "on a radical approach – to *follow* the book rather than depart from it."[2] So Huston began laying the story out in scenes, simply putting the novel into script form. He didn't get far, though, because he was suddenly called away by Warner's story department to work on a script for the pro-war film *Sergeant York*. But before leaving, Huston handed the novel to his secretary and told her to continue laying it out in scenes as he had been doing.[3] He intended to begin the actual script revisions when he returned.

Then, as Huston put it, "the damndest thing happened."[4] It was company policy for secretaries to send copies of their work to their bosses, so a copy of the secretary's manuscript got into Warner's hands. Warner thought the reformatted novel was the final script, called Huston in, and said, "I just read it and it's great. You've really captured the flavor of the book. Now go shoot it with my blessing."[5]

The term "film novel" comes from Carl Dreyer, the acclaimed Danish film director, who, in 1922, urged novelists to write scripts in the form of novels. Other terms used for "film novel" since then include scenario novel, movie novel, and cinema novel. The American novelist and poet Jack Kerouac used yet another term: "Bookmovie is the movie in

**Of Mice and Men, 1939**

words, the visual American form."[6] Film novels are short – about 30,000 words – and take about as long to read as a feature film takes to watch. The description, dialogue, and narration of a film novel can simply be lifted out and used as the description, dialogue, and voice-over narration for a script.

After the publication of *The Maltese Falcon* came other film novels, such as *Sanctuary* by William Faulkner (1931), *Of Mice and Men* by John Steinbeck (1937), *The Chips Are Down* by Jean-Paul Sartre (1948), and *The Misfits* by Arthur Miller (1961). All were filmed shortly after they were written. At Brigham Young University, where I teach, undergraduates have begun writing and publishing film novels, like Gordon Law's *My People* – a film novel that critics have called "literarily sophisticated" and "probing and mature."[7]

This book is a primer on writing film novels. It will help you understand them and get you started in writing them, whether you are a beginning novelist, a seasoned writer crossing over into the world of writing scripts/film novels, or a creative writing teacher trying out a new way to launch your students. The first three chapters are warmups: they explore the history of film novels and the techniques used in writing them, and they get you organized, focused, and ready to write one yourself.

In the first chapter, you will read about the history and style of the modern novels that led up to film novels, from Gustave Flaubert's *Madame Bovary* to James Joyce's *Ulysses*. You will see how modern novels culminated in film novels. You will also see how film novels collectively include everything other novels do – not only dialogue and description, but narration, flashbacks, moments of imagination, and interior thoughts. And you will see how film novels use these various elements in ways that always allow readers to picture and hear scenes in their heads. You will also learn how to set up a competent team of readers and/or writers to work with.

In the second chapter, you will learn the history of film novels themselves. Along the way, you will learn why writing a film novel is so much more satisfying than just writing a script, why they are more likely to be published than scripts, why they are more likely to be read and filmed by filmmakers, and why they are much more likely than other novels to be filmed as written. You will also practice writing scenes like those in successful film novels, and you will select a story you want to turn into a screenplay and film novel. The story you pick may be one you have come up with yourself, or it may be an existing screenplay or novel you want to rewrite.

In the third chapter, the most philosophically demanding one, you will discover how subtext in a film novel – what we read between the lines – engages us and why film novels with subtext can be the most vivid and engaging novels written today. You will learn about the philosophical concept of generosity and the role of generosity in writing subtext. You will also begin doing research for your story.

In the next five chapters, the most labor-intensive ones, you will summarize and then write your screenplay and film novel. The approach is step by step, moving from a one-sentence pitch, to a five- to six-page synopsis, to a fifteen- to twenty-page scenario, to a script with summarized dialogue, to a script with actual dialogue, then finally to the novel itself. But the approach isn't formulaic: you won't be asked, for example, to write three acts instead of five as in a Shakespearean play. You won't be asked to write plot-driven or character-driven stories. You will instead focus on integrating all the core elements typically taught in short-story courses – plot, character development, theme, style. For a short novel is simply a long story. In the final chapter, you will look beyond writing into the sphere of filming. You will explore the fundamentals of turning your filmic novel into a literary film.

Each chapter starts with an introduction and assignments. After you read them, you will write questions you would like answered by the end of the chapter. Then as you read the rest of the chapter, you will be an active participant in trying to answer your questions yourself. Proceeding in this way, you will always have a reason for what you are learning. At the end of each chapter, you will see the work of a writing team doing the same step-by-step assignments you are doing. (Some of their work isn't in the text but is posted online at www.greatcinemanow. com/filmnovelist.)

If you spend eight hours on each of the weekly assignments at the beginning of the chapters and have a good group of friends to help you along, by the end of fifteen weeks you will have written a draft of a screenplay and a novel and filmed a scene. If you want to go through the chapters in the more traditional order of scriptwriting, novel writing, and filming, you can start by jumping into the scriptwriting assignments (Chapters 4 to 6). Then, with script in hand, you can turn your script into a novel (Chapters 1 to 3 and 8) and film a scene (Chapter 9). Going either route, straight through or roundabout, you will be ready to talk to a book publisher and a film producer. You will be on your way to becoming a film novelist.

## Student Writing Group

This is Madeleine, your past student, reporting back for duty. I am excited to work through these now much-refined assignments. Having been through two internship semesters with you, I can anticipate (and bite my fingernails over) the difficulty of what is before me, but that stress is of the good variety.

The final semester of my internship with you was the highlight of my college experience, not only because I was working with talented, tolerant people, but because the process of writing a script brought challenges that opened my red-rimmed eyes to self-discovery.

So now that I am on board, I am determined to be the best film novelist in the universe, embracing my destiny. I greet you with a somewhat goofy smile and an awe-inspiring wave of the hand. Onward to script-ory!

# Stage One: Warming Up

# Sentences

In this chapter you will read about the landmark novels that led up to the creation of film novels. You will learn how film novels and scripts have basically the same content, just a different format. You will learn how movie scripts indicate solely what the audience is to see or hear on screen; and you will learn how they intersperse scene description throughout dialogue and voice-over narration so that the scenes can be visualized while being heard. You will learn how novels achieve the same effect when written filmically. In the process, you will learn how to write sentences for film novels and screenplays.

### Week One

1. Read the introduction for this chapter and the assignments, and write questions that arise for you. Then read the rest of the chapter, and write your answers. Here are some sample questions you could ask and try to answer for this chapter:

   - What exactly does a film novel do that a normal novel doesn't?
   - Movie scripts consist of what we can see and hear. So how can they convey characters' thoughts?
   - What does it mean to "intersperse scene description throughout dialogue and voice-over narration"?
   - What does it mean for novels to be "written filmically"?

2. Read some stories suggested in the appendix. To get a feel for the sentences in these stories, copy down four of them that you like and categorize them as sentences of scene description, dialogue, interior monologue, narration, or a mix of them (e.g., a mix of scene description and dialogue).
3. Now write four sentences yourself, ones you might use in a film novel scene you would like to write. Indicate the type of each sentence you write—that is, whether it is scene description, dialogue, interior monologue, narration, or a mix of them.
4. Pick the writing team you will be working with.

### Glossary

| | |
|---|---|
| **scene** | What happens during one continuous stretch of time and location[1] |
| **scene description** | Words describing the sights and sounds in scenes (except dialogue), including the action |
| **dialogue** | Words that characters say aloud |
| **interior monologue** | Words that characters say in their heads |
| **narration** | Words of a story other than scene description, dialogue, and interior monologue, like exposition and summary |
| **exposition** | Narration of background information |
| **narrative summary** | Narration summarizing actions or habitual actions |
| **film novel** | A novel of about 30,000 words of scene description interspersed in dialogue or interior monologue or narration |

In 1919 Samuel Goldwyn issued a massive thirty-two-page insert for two major Hollywood trade magazines. It was, in his words, "the largest and most elaborate insert ever used in the industry."[2] But its length wasn't the

**Samuel Goldwyn**

only thing that made it groundbreaking. Rather than simply using the space to advertise his new films, as would have been customary, Goldwyn was actually announcing the formation of a new body of writers to be called "Eminent Authors." Goldwin intended to hire novelists to write stories for him and playwrights to help with the dialogue. Having been recently dropped as a partner from Famous Players-Lasky (an agency that hired famous actors and actresses), Goldwyn took the idea of employing well-known talent and made it his own. As if to one-up his previous partners, Goldwyn began hiring the services of famous authors.

These authors granted Goldwyn a ninety-day option to buy the film rights to their upcoming works. If Goldwyn chose to film their stories, they would receive "one-third of the film's earnings" with "a $10,000 advance" from those earnings.[3] The terms were generous in 1919, but unfortunately, the effort failed. The writers couldn't seem to understand the needs of film, and Goldwyn couldn't seem to convincingly explain those needs to them. Goldwyn complained:

> The great trouble with the usual author is that he approaches the camera with some fixed literary ideal and he cannot compromise with the motion picture viewpoint. . . . This attitude brought many writers whom I had assembled into almost immediate conflict with our scenario department.[4]

What Goldwyn and his eminent authors lacked was a shared vision of the type of novel suitable for film and an understanding of the evolution of the modern novel. They didn't know that within the previous 60 years the style of the modern novel had been evolving from traditional storytelling toward a literary version of scripts. These literary scripts would soon be called film novels, and reading one of them would be like watching a movie in your head.

But, of course, Goldwyn and his writers couldn't be expected to have understood that literary development. They were too close to it, and it hadn't been articulated well yet. Today we can understand it, and this understanding can help writers and producers work together in the way Goldwyn had hoped for.

So let's look at how modern novels moved from traditional storytelling toward film scripts. Scripts consist of one scene after another, but traditional storytelling—the type we find, for example, in the Bible—consists of exposition, then narrative summary, then scenes.[5] Take, for example, the story of Naaman, the Syrian leper, in the Bible. First, we find a little exposition introducing Naaman:

> Now Naaman, captain of the host of the king of Syria, was a great man with his master, and honourable, because by him the LORD had given deliverance unto Syria: he was also a mighty man in valour, but he was a leper.[6]

A scriptwriter wouldn't begin a script like that. Instead, he would start with a scene of Naaman doing something, and perhaps use exposition as voice-over to explain the man's backstory. In the Bible, after the little bit of exposition, we get a narrative summary:

> And the Syrians had gone out by companies, and had brought away captive out of the land of Israel a little maid; and she waited on Naaman's wife.[7]

In a script, a writer would show the little girl doing something, and maybe use narrative summary as voice over. In the story of Naaman, it isn't until after the exposition and narrative summary that we finally get the first scene, a single line of dialogue:

> And she said unto her mistress, "Would God my lord were with the prophet that is in Samaria! for he would recover him of his leprosy."[8]

This traditional pattern of exposition, narrative summary, then scene dominated seventeenth- and eighteenth-century literature and remained strong in the early nineteenth century. We find the pattern, for example, in *Don Quixote, Tom Jones, Emma, The Red and the Black*, and *Eugene Onegin*.[9] But the passages of exposition and narrative summary in these novels are much longer than those in the Bible.

Cervantes' *Don Quixote*, for instance, begins with a long passage of exposition introducing the gentleman from La Mancha:

> In a village of La Mancha, the name of which I have no desire to recall, there lived not so long ago one of those gentlemen who always have a lance in the rack, an ancient buckler, a skinny nag, and a greyhound for the chase. A stew with more beef than mutton in it, chopped meat for the evening meal, scraps for a Saturday, lentils on Friday, and a young pigeon as a special delicacy for Sunday, went to account for three-quarters of his income. The rest of it he laid out on a broadcloth greatcoat and velvet stockings for feast days, with slippers to match, while the other days of the week he cut a figure in a suit of the finest homespun. Living with him were a housekeeper in her forties, a niece who was not yet twenty, and a lad of the field and market-place who saddled his horse for him and wielded the pruning knife.[10]

**Cervantes**

A second paragraph of exposition follows, and then comes narrative summary—preliminary information summarizing what the gentleman did, and tended to do, before he began his first adventure:

> You may know, then, that the aforesaid gentleman, on those occasions when he was at leisure, which was most of the year around, was in the habit of reading books of chivalry with such pleasure and devotion as to lead him almost wholly to forget the life of a hunter and even the administration of his estate. So great was his curiosity and infatuation in this regard that he even sold many acres of tillable land in order to be able to buy and read the books that he loved, and he would carry home with him as many of them as he could obtain.[11]

The summary of the man's preparation for his adventure continues to the end of the first chapter. Then finally, in the third sentence of the second chapter, the first scene begins with a description of action:

> Donning all his armor, mounting Rocinante, adjusting his ill-contrived helmet, bracing his shield on his arm, and taking up his lance, he sallied forth by the back gate of his stable yard into the open countryside.[12]

The novel's narrative strategy is traditional, like the Bible's, only Cervantes moves much more slowly from exposition to summary to scene than the biblical writers do.

Traditional storytelling lasted into the mid-nineteenth century. Then a French novelist, Gustave Flaubert—who thought all other books were dwarfs beside *Don Quixote*[13]—led novelists away from traditional storytelling toward the more scenic modes of modern novels.

### Flaubert

Gustave Flaubert was born in Rouen, France, in 1821. As a child, he regularly attended plays in his hometown, where he saw most of the famous actors from Paris.[14] At the age of eight, he was writing his own plays and decided to become a playwright. A year later, inspired by *Don Quixote*, he decided instead to become a novelist, but he continued to produce classical and modern plays in his home with his friends and family. By the age of 14, he had written a number of plays and stories.[15] Six years later, away at school in Paris, he maintained his interest in the stage and wrote several more plays. During that same year, he also finished his first novel.[16] When he was 44 and well established as a novelist, he staged one of his plays. But

**Gustave Flaubert**

disappointed with its reception, he canceled the play a few days after its opening.[17]

By then Flaubert had written the novel generally considered his masterpiece, *Madame Bovary* (1856). "Flaubert saw his novel as a succession of scenes," his biographer Enid Starkie explains. "He called [the scenes] *tableaux*." He wrote "many successive scenarios, as he called them, which helped him to make clear to himself what he wanted to say."[18] This theatrical way of thinking about novels, Starkie suggests, grew out of Flaubert's "early interest in the stage" and "the fact that his first literary efforts were mostly in the form of plays."[19] If the modern novel was created by Flaubert, as is often claimed, it was created by one who thought in terms of *scenes*.[20]

The first chapter of *Madame Bovary* begins not with a traditional expository introduction of the main characters and their setting, but with a scene that takes up half the chapter. Throughout the novel, Flaubert relies heavily on scenes like those found in film scripts. In the following, for example, he simply describes the sights and sounds of a scene:

> Emma made her toilet with the fastidious care of an actress on her debut. She did her hair according to the directions of the hairdresser, and put on the barege dress spread out upon the bed. Charles's trousers were tight across the belly.
>
> "My trouser-straps will be rather awkward for dancing," he said.
>
> "Dancing?" repeated Emma.
>
> "Yes!"
>
> "Why, you must be mad! They would make fun of you; keep your place. Besides, it is more becoming for a doctor," she added.
>
> Charles was silent. He walked up and down waiting for Emma to finish dressing. He saw her from behind in the glass between two lights. Her black eyes seemed blacker than ever. Her hair, undulating towards the ears, shone with a blue luster, a rose in her chignon trembled on its mobile stalk, with artificial dewdrops on the tip of the leaves. She wore a gown of pale saffron trimmed with three bouquets of pompon roses mixed with green.
>
> Charles came and kissed her on her shoulder.
>
> "Let me alone!" she said; "you are mussing me."
>
> One could hear the flourish of the violin and the notes of a horn. She went downstairs trying not to run.[21]

Rewriting such a scene in script form is simple. We set the scene in the interior of a bedroom, in the evening, and begin with a sequence of short shots. (Note that a script is written in present tense and the dialogue is indented an additional one inch from each side.[22] Written this way, each page of script amounts to roughly one minute of screen time.)

INT. BEDROOM—EVENING

Emma makes her toilet [dresses and grooms] with
the fastidious care of an actress on her debut.
She does her hair according to the [written] direc-
tions of the hairdresser.

She puts on the barege dress spread out upon the
bed.

Charles's trousers are tight across the belly.

> CHARLES
> My trouser-straps will be rather
> awkward for dancing.

> EMMA
> Dancing?

> CHARLES
> Yes!

> EMMA
> Why, you must be mad! They would
> make fun of you; keep your place.
> Besides, it is more becoming for
> a doctor.

Charles is silent. He walks up and down waiting for
Emma to finish dressing. He sees her from behind in
the glass between two lights. Her black eyes seem
blacker than ever. Her hair, undulating towards
the ears, shines with a blue luster, a rose in her
chignon trembles on its mobile stalk, with artifi-
cial dewdrops on the tip of the leaves. She wears
a gown of pale saffron trimmed with three bouquets
of pompon roses mixed with green.

Charles comes and kisses her on her shoulder.

> EMMA
> Let me alone! You are mussing
> me.

One can hear the flourish of the violin and the
notes of a horn.

```
INT. TOP OF STAIRS—EVENING

She goes downstairs, trying not to run.
```

In place of narrative summary, Flaubert often uses brief descriptions of scenes, one after another, like this:

> He went out with the laborers, drove away with clods of earth the ravens that were flying about. He ate blackberries along the hedges, minded the geese with a long switch, went haymaking during harvest, ran about in the woods, played hop-scotch under the church porch on rainy days, and at great fêtes begged the beadle to let him toll the bells, that he might hang all his weight on the long rope and feel himself borne upward by it in its swing.[23]

Filmmakers call such a sequence of short, disconnected scenes a *montage sequence*. We can reformat the preceding montage sequence in script format like this:

```
MONTAGE

—He goes out with the laborers.
—He drives away with clods of earth the ravens
 that are flying about.
—He eats blackberries along the hedges.
—He minds the geese with a long switch.
—He goes haymaking during harvest.
—He runs about in the woods.
—He plays hopscotch under the church porch on
 rainy days.
—At great fêtes, he begs the beadle to let him toll
 the bells, that he may hang all his weight on the
 long rope and feel himself borne upward by it in
 its swing.
```

Flaubert also uses interior monologue in scenes. Here is an example:

> Sitting on the grass that she dug up with little prods of her sunshade, Emma repeated to herself, "Good heavens! Why did I marry?"[24]

Filmmakers could convey Emma's unspoken words with voice-over, abbreviated as (V.O.), during a close-up shot of Emma thinking but not speaking. Here is how we would rewrite the scene in script format:

```
EXT. HILLSIDE-DAY

Emma sits on the grass that she digs up with
little prods of her sunshade.
                    EMMA (V.O.)
          Good heavens! Why did I marry?
```

Besides interior monologue, Flaubert uses narration interspersed with
enough scene description for readers to keep picturing scenes. Here is an
example:

From respect, or from a sort of sensuality that made him carry on
his investigations slowly, Charles had not yet opened the secret
drawer of a rosewood desk which Emma had generally used. One
day, however, he sat down before it, turned the key, and pressed the
spring. All Leon's letters were there. There could be no doubt this
time. He devoured them to the very last, ransacked every corner,
all the furniture, all the drawers, behind the walls, sobbing, crying
aloud, distraught, mad. He found a box and broke it open with a
kick. Rodolphe's portrait flew full in his face in the midst of the overturned love letters.[25]

This passage consists of scene description with narration. We could cast the
narration as Charles's voice-over—his reflections years afterwards (or we
could cast it as the third-person thoughts of someone other than Charles).
Here is an example of how that would be done:

```
INT. HOUSE-DAY

                    CHARLES (V.O.)
          From respect, or from a sort of
          sensuality that made me carry
          on my investigations slowly,
          I had not yet opened the secret
          drawer of a rosewood desk which
          Emma had generally used.

Charles considers the desk. He sits down before
it, turns the key, and presses the spring.

                    CHARLES (V.O.)
          All Leon's letters were there.
          There could be no doubt this
          time.
```

# Sentences

He devours them to the very last, ransacks every corner, all the furniture, all the drawers, behind the walls, sobbing, crying aloud, distraught, mad.

He finds a box and breaks it open with a kick. Rodolphe's portrait flies full in his face in the midst of the overturned love letters.

In this script, as in all scripts, the scene description comes before or after voice-over or dialogue. But in movies, the sights and sounds of a scene occur simultaneously, not sequentially. Yet if they are sufficiently close together in a script or a novel, the reader experiences them as if they were occurring simultaneously. When scene description occurs frequently enough in a scene for readers to keep picturing the scene, the scene description is said to be interspersed within the scene.

Besides alternating sentences of scene description and narration, Flaubert also mixes scene description and narration within sentences. Here is an example (I have italicized the scene description within the narration):

*When she was thirteen*, her father himself took her to town to place her in the convent. *They stopped at an inn* in the St. Gervais quarter, where, *at their supper, they used painted plates* that set forth the story of Mademoiselle de la Vallière. The explanatory legends, *chipped here and there by the scratching of knives*, all glorified religion, the tenderness of the heart, and the pomps of court.[26]

In a film, the entire passage would be read as a voice-over, and the visual parts would be shown on screen as a montage of brief scenes. Here is how we could cast the passage in script format:

```
                EMMA (V.O.)
           (as per voice-over)
    When I was thirteen, my father
    himself took me to town to place
    me in a convent. We stopped at
    an inn in the St. Gervais quar-
    ter, where, at our supper, we
    used painted plates that set
    forth the story of Mademoiselle
    de la Vallière. The explanatory
    legends, chipped here and there
    by the scratching of knives,
```

> all glorified religion, the ten-
> derness of the heart, and the
> pomps of court.

The phrase "as per voice-over" indicates that the scenes described in the voice-over are to be shown on screen. Such visual narration is used extensively as voice-over in films like *Barry Lyndon* and How *Green Was My Valley.*[27]

Because of Flaubert's use of scene description, much of the narration in *Madame Bovary* can be reformatted in script form. But not all of the novel's narration can be reformatted.[28] Flaubert didn't *always* write scenically—he didn't always engage readers in picturing scenes. But he did write much more scenically than novelists before him.

Flaubert's move toward scenes exerted a tremendous influence on subsequent writers. Spiegel writes, "In 1857 Flaubert published *Madame Bovary*, and the influence of this book upon the literary generation of Joyce's youth and, in fact, upon practically all subsequent literary generations—including the present one—cannot be overestimated."[29] Writers who latched onto Flaubert's style of writing novels in scenes included the so-called realists[30]—Tolstoy, Turgenev, Chekhov, de Maupassant, Conrad, Hardy, Howells, James, Crane, and the early Joyce—who thought of Flaubert as one of the few masters of the novel. Joyce memorized whole pages of Flaubert's works.[31] Other writers who picked up on the idea were the so-called naturalists—Zola, Bennet, Moore, Norris, London, and Dreiser.[32]

**Barry Lyndon, 1975**

## Zola, Chekhov, and James

In the late nineteenth century, other novelists began to write even more scenically than Flaubert. Emile Zola used scenes in his novels more often than Flaubert, but not always. He didn't always use enough description for readers to continuously picture scenes.

In 1890 Anton Chekhov, the Russian storywriter and playwright, wrote *The Duel*, a novella of over 30,000 words, consisting mostly of scenes. Donald Rayfield writes, "*The Duel* is virtually drama transposed into storytelling. . . . Even the descriptive passages are condensed into no more than an occasional dozen words, and it requires little to convert them into stage effects."[33] The novelist Nabokov writes that Chekhov's "qualities as a playwright are merely his qualities as a writer of long short stories."[34] In other words, his best plays were simply short novels to be enacted on stage.

Henry James' interest in scenes, like Flaubert's and Chekhov's, came from the theater. In 1890, when James was 47 and midway into a successful career as a novelist, he turned to writing for the stage. He had some success when the dramatization of his novel *The American* was produced. After five years, he returned to writing novels, which he began writing more scenically. In every passage of narration, he gives his readers a glimpse of scenes, but not always enough of a look at them to keep his readers picturing them. In *The Ambassadors* (1903), for example—his favorite of his novels—he puts his lead character in a park, where he reflects, mostly without accompanying scene description, for seven pages before the author returns to describing the park.

Though Flaubert, Zola, Chekhov, and James wrote in scenes, they seemed to have been thinking theatrically, as if writing plays. They often wrote enough

The Duel, 2009

**Anton Chekov**

description for their readers to at least initially picture scenes, as playwrights often do, but not always enough for them to continue picturing them, as scriptwriters do. Not until the advent of film do we see novelists mimicking the motion of a camera's changing view of a scene by offering enough scene description for readers to continually picture new aspects of each scene as it unfolds.

### Joyce

The first twentieth-century novelist to write filmic chapters one after another was James Joyce in his novel *Ulysses*. One critic writes, "It is no exaggeration to

**James Joyce**

say that [Joyce's] *Ulysses* [1922] contains equivalents for almost every conceivable filmic technique," including cross-cuts, fades, and dissolves, even slow motion.

As a young man, Joyce saw films in Paris and elsewhere on the continent. In 1909, when he was 21, he "persuaded [an Italian] movie syndicate to open [movie] theaters in Ireland, commencing with Dublin, and to hire him as [an] advance agent."[35] Dublin's Volta Theatre opened with an acclaimed program of Italian films. After ten days of supervision, Joyce left a co-owner of the movie theater in charge. Within a year, "in large measure [due] to the novelist's neglect of the operation—the Dublin theater failed."[36] Still, Joyce continued to frequent movie theaters. In the 1920s he was a regular patron at movies. A friend recalls Joyce speaking enthusiastically about films: "As he talked . . . I seemed to see him in a darkened theater, the great prose master absorbed in camera technique."[37]

The initial chapters of *Ulysses* just describe the sights and sounds of scenes, leaving narration and interior monologue for later chapters. The novel begins like this:

> Stately, plump Buck Mulligan came from the stairhead, bearing a bowl of lather on which a mirror and a razor lay crossed. A yellow dressing-gown, ungirdled, was sustained gently behind him on the mild morning air. He held the bowl aloft and intoned:
> —*Introibo ad altare Dei.*
> Halted, he peered down the dark winding stairs and called out coarsely:
> —Come up, Kinch! Come up, you fearful jesuit!
> Solemnly he came forward and mounted the round gunrest. He faced about and blessed gravely thrice the tower, the surrounding land and the awaking mountains. Then, catching sight of Stephen Dedalus, he bent towards him and made rapid crosses in the air, gurgling in his throat and shaking his head. Stephen Dedalus, displeased and sleepy, leaned his arms on the top of the staircase and looked coldly at the shaking gurgling face that blessed him, equine in its length, and at the light untonsured hair, grained and hued like pale oak.[38]

Later in *Ulysses*, we find Joyce using interior monologue interspersed within scene description:

> —Look at yourself, he said, you dreadful bard!
> Stephen bent forward and peered at the mirror held out to him, cleft by a crooked crack. Hair on end. As he and others see me. Who chose this face for me? This dogsbody to rid of vermin. It asks me too.[39]

We see Stephen looking in the mirror, and we see his hair on end in the mirror and hear his inner thoughts: "As he and others see me. Who chose this face for me? This dogsbody to rid of vermin. It asks me too."

The following longer passage, about a milk woman, includes narration:

> —How much, sir? asked the old woman.
> —A quart, Stephen said.

He watched her pour into the measure and thence into the jug rich white milk, not hers. Old shrunken paps. She poured again a measureful and a tilly. Old and secret she had entered from a morning world, maybe a messenger. She praised the goodness of the milk, pouring it out. Crouching by a patient cow at daybreak in the lush field, a witch on her toadstool, her wrinkled fingers quick at the squirting dugs. They lowed about her whom they knew, dewsilky cattle. Silk of the kine and poor old woman, names given her in old times. A wandering crone, lowly form of an immortal serving her conqueror and her gay betrayer, their common cuckquean, a messenger from the secret morning. To serve or to upbraid, whether he could not tell: but scorned to beg her favour.

—It is indeed, ma'am, Buck Mulligan said, pouring milk into their cups.

—Taste it, sir, she said.

He drank at her bidding.[40]

In this passage, Stephen's poetic voice-over apparently alludes to "poor, sterile, subjected Ireland."[41] We can recast the passage in script format like this:

```
INT. HOUSE—DAY

                    OLD WOMAN
          How much, sir?

                    STEPHEN
          A quart.

He watches her pour into the measure and thence
into the jug rich white milk, not hers.

                    STEPHEN (V.O.)
          Old shrunken paps.

She pours again a measureful and a tilly.

                    STEPHEN (V.O.)
          Old and secret she has entered
          from a morning world, maybe a
          messenger.

She praises the goodness of the milk, pouring it
out.
```

EXT. FIELD—DAY

Crouching by a patient cow at daybreak in the lush
field, a witch on her toadstool, her wrinkled fingers quick at the squirting dugs. They low about
her whom they know, dewsilky cattle.

                         STEPHEN (V.O.)
              Silk of the kine and poor old
              woman, names given her in old
              times. A wandering crone, lowly
              form of an immortal serving her
              conqueror and her gay betrayer,
              their common cuckquean, a mes-
              senger from the secret morning.
              To serve or to upbraid, whether
              I can not tell: but scorn to
              beg her favor.

INT. HOUSE—DAY

                         BUCK
              (pouring milk into
              their cups)
              It is indeed, ma'am.

                         OLD WOMAN
              Taste it, sir.

He drinks at her bidding.

The preceding script format is not all that alien to *Ulysses* itself. Over a
fourth of the novel is written as script, complete with voice-over.

In scenes like these last ones, Joyce masterfully keeps us attentive to a character's inner life. We see the character viewing a scene—"He watched her pour
into the measure and thence into the jug rich white milk, not hers." Then we
hear the character's reflection—"Old sunken paps." Then we see the character
viewing the scene again—"She poured again a measureful and a tilly." Then
we see the character imagining the witch in the field. And while we watch her,
we hear the character's reflections about Ireland—which is symbolized by the
witch—"lowly form of an immortal serving her conqueror." Joyce requires us
to track a character's rapidly changing mental activities.

Joyce's style is like that of montage in film. As one critic puts it, Joyce
perfected "novelistic equivalents" of montage.[42] He not only juxtaposes
diverse scenes (like present and imagined scenes), but he does the novelistic

**Sergei Eisenstein**

equivalent of laying voice-over on top of these scenes. As a result, readers understand Joyce by attending to a visual as well as an aural track of information. Readers must synthesize the two tracks to understand the text.

The pioneering film theorist and director Sergei Eisenstein praised Joyce for his use of inner monologues:

Literature's most brilliant achievement in this field has been the immortal "inner monologues" of Leopold Bloom in *Ulysses.* When Joyce and I met in Paris, he was intensely interested in my plans for the inner film-monologue.[43]

At their meeting in Joyce's apartment in 1930, "Joyce read aloud passages of *Ulysses*" to Eisenstein and "expressed [interest in seeing] Eisenstein's films *Potemkin* and *October*."[44] After the meeting, Joyce told friends that if anyone were to film *Ulysses*, it would have to be someone like Eisenstein.[45] Only someone with Eisenstein's creativity could make the new type of film to which Joyce's novel pointed.

*Ulysses* was filmed, but not by Eisenstein, after Joyce's death—many say unsatisfactorily. But the novel helped writers appreciate what they could learn from film. *Ulysses* explored the possibilities of filmic writing so thoroughly that Joyce became, as one critic puts it, "a guide" to a "new breed of fiction writer."[46] "The history of the novel after 1922—the year *Ulysses* appeared—is to a large extent that of the development of a cinematic imagination in novelists and their [often] ambivalent attempt[s] to come to grips with the 'liveliest art' of the twentieth century."[47]

## Your Writing Team

As your historical understanding of the rise of film novels grows, you will want to begin thinking about writing your own script and novel. That includes thinking about your writing team. Most people think that a script or novel is written by one person. But actually, most scripts, at least those that are filmed, are written by several writers. One writer may write the first draft of a script, but once a producer buys it, or options to buy it, the producer is free to involve one writer after another. He may say to a writer, "Thanks for the great story," and then ask another writer to restructure it. And he may then say to that writer, "Thanks for working out such a good structure," and then ask someone else to redo the dialogue.

There is an alternative to this method of passing scripts from one writer to another: involve other writers from the start—one writer or several, perhaps even a class of student writers. Television series are written by several writers. They work on various aspects of a script, like different lines of action for separate characters, and then submit their work to a head writer, who pulls everything together into a final draft. The key to working with a group of other writers is to have clear responsibilities and to establish early who will pull the final drafts of various parts of the writing together.

But you may want to work alone. Even so you will need to have in place a group of writers who are willing to read drafts of your work and give you their candid, helpful responses. The key is to get their feedback early in the writing process.

If you are working on a project for a producer who has brought you a script to rework and turn into a film novel, you can work alone or with a group, but you will need to pass your work by the producer often. Be sure to show your producer your best work—don't show him all your drafts, your dead ends, your problems. Show him your work after you have passed it by your readers and received a good response. Then be prepared to explain what you are trying to do when he raises concerns and be ready to make changes when he requests them.

## The Next Chapter

In this first chapter, you have looked at the style of modern writing that is used in film novels: description of scenes interspersed within dialogue, narration, and interior monologue. This is writing you can transfer directly to scripts as description, dialogue, and voice-over. You have also thought about, and hopefully put together, your writing team. In the next chapter, you will see how this style of writing has been used in actual film novels.

## Student Writing Group

### Week One

1. Read the introduction for this chapter and the assignments, and write questions that arise for you. Then read the rest of the chapter, and write your answers.

   *Why should my writing be filmic? Plenty of novels—not guided to completion by this book—have been successfully filmed. Right? This chapter suggests that there is a developing method to novel writing. Over time, novels have become more and more filmic, which does say a lot about what modern audiences expect—they like a novel that is written filmically so that they can experience the story with their senses and imagination. This book teaches you how to be a writer who can create just such a novel.*

2. Read some stories suggested in the appendix. To get a feel for the sentences in these stories, copy down four of them that you like and categorize them as sentences of scene description, dialogue, interior monologue, narration, or a mix of them (e.g., a mix of scene description and dialogue).

I read "Say Yes" by Tobias Wolff. Thereafter, I added two *f*'s to the end of my name, for classiness—Madeleineff. My favorite sentences:

She was piling dishes on the drainboard at a terrific rate, just swiping at them with the cloth. Many of them were greasy, and there were flecks of food between the tines of the forks. [scene description]

He hoped that she appreciated how quickly he had come to her aid. He'd acted out of concern for her, with no thought of getting anything in return, but now the thought occurred to him that it would be a nice gesture on her part not to start up that conversation again, as he was tired of it. [interior monologue]

3. Now write four sentences yourself, ones you might use in a film novel scene you would like to write. Indicate the type of each sentence you write—that is, whether it is scene description, dialogue, interior monologue, narration, or a mix of them.

Where's the trust? Can't a guy just be born to win?" he asked, pushing some of his winnings behind him. [dialogue, scene description]

Charlotte couldn't hear the laughter anymore. [scene description] She knew her brother was hiding from her, but she also knew that there wasn't a thing she could do about it. [interior monologue]

4. Pick the writing team you will be working with.

After I proved how splendiferously I could work with Melanie Henderson this last semester, I decided to team up with her on this project. I'll be venturing through the first three chapters solo. But once I reach Chapter 4, Mel will ninja-appear, and together we will conquer our script.

# Scenes

In the last chapter, you learned about the types of sentences that can be used in film novels. In this chapter, you will see how such sentences have actually been used in past film novels and how they could be used in future ones. Then you will select a subject for your film novel.

## Week Two

1. Read the introduction and assignments, and write your questions. Then read the chapter, and write your answers.
2. Read a film novel suggested in the appendix, and copy down some scenes you like.
3. Now write a film novel scene yourself, using some of the sentences you wrote in the last chapter.
4. Find a story that you (as an individual or as a group, perhaps as a class) would like to turn into a screenplay and film novel. Or find a script you would like to rewrite and then turn into a film novel.

## Glossary

| | |
|---|---|
| **flashback** | A scene that shows the past before returning to the present |
| **flash-forward** | A scene that shows the future before returning to the present |
| **imagined scene** | A scene that shows what a character is imagining |

| **linear film novel** | A film novel without flashbacks, flash-forwards, or imagined scenes |
| **simple film novel** | A linear film novel without narration or interior monologue |
| **complex film novel** | A film novel that is neither linear nor simple |

In 1922, the same year Joyce's *Ulysses* appeared, Carl Dreyer wrote an article about film novels. He was then nine years into his film career, had directed four films—three based on novels and one on a short story—and had written film scripts for 23 films, almost half of them based on novels, none on plays. Now he was looking again for novels to film.[1] Dreyer explained in his article that filmmakers were right

**Carl Dreyer**

to look for novels to film: novels have a life of their own, outside of the filmmaker's world, a life that gives filmmakers a cause worth serving.[2] Dreyer called the novels he was looking for "film manuscripts" in "the form of the novel," or "film novels."[3]

Dreyer explained that he wasn't looking for a new style of writing, just a more consistent use of a style that already existed.[4] As an example, he quoted a passage from a novel by J. P. Jacobsen:

**J. P. Jacobsen**

One night candles were being made in the servants' hall of Tjele. Marie stood at the copper mold, which was sunken down in a hay-filled vat, and immersed the wicks that the scullery girl, Ane Trinderup, Søren's niece, let drip off into a yellow earthenware dish. The cook took the platters, picked them up and hung them under the candle table, and took away the candles when they had become thick enough. At the servants' hall table, Søren Ladefoged sat looking on; he was dressed in a red cloth cap that was decorated with gold braids and black feathers; a silver pitcher stood in front of him with mead, and he was eating from a big piece of roast that he sliced with his clasp knife on a small pewter plate. He ate with great sedateness, drank from the mug, and responded now and then to Marie's smiling nod with a slow, appreciative movement of his head.

She asked him if he was seated comfortably.

More or less so.

So it was best that Ane go into the maid's room and get a pillow for him.

So she then did this, but not without making quite a few signs to the other girl behind Marie's back.

Wouldn't Søren like a piece of cake?

Yes, that wouldn't be so bad.

Marie took a wick spindle and went for the cake but stayed away rather long.

She was barely outside the door when both girls started to roar with laughter, just as if previously arranged.

Søren frowned angrily at them.[5]

This passage, consisting of scene description and indirect discourse, could easily be rewritten in script format.

In his article, Dreyer urged both scriptwriters and novelists to write film novels. To scriptwriters, he explained that film novels are more artistically satisfying to write than scripts, because they are more complete. And because they are more complete, they are more likely to be published than scripts and more likely to be read and filmed by filmmakers. Filmmakers are eager for novels to film, because they know novels have been approved by publishers and already have audiences. To novelists, he explained that film novels can be transferred to film more directly, with fewer changes, than other types of novels, and yet, as the above passage from Jacobsen shows, film novels needn't be radically different from other novels. They can include everything other novels do, as long as readers can keep picturing scenes.

Dreyer apparently failed to find scriptwriters or novelists answering his call for film novels, for in late 1922 he made his first film based on a play. Of his next five films, only one was based on a novel. Two others were based on original film scripts, one on a play, and one on two short stories. By 1933, a year after he'd shot his first sound film, he had given up on novels.

Since I define the real sound film as a film capable of fascinating by its psychological content, its story, and its remarks alone, without help from exaggerated sound effects, musical accompaniment, and inserted musical numbers, the psychological play is probably to be considered the most suitable material, on the condition, though, that the idea of the drama, its *raw material*, is extricated from the form of the play and transformed into film.[6]

All four of Dreyer's next, and last, feature films were adaptations of plays. While Dreyer was looking for film novels, Americans across the Atlantic had begun writing them. These American "film manuscripts" in "the form of the novel" were short novels, composed almost entirely of dialogue and scene description, though some of them were beginning to use narration. They were instances of what some French critics, like Claude-Edmonde Magny, writing in 1948, more loosely called "the American novel."[7] By this Magny meant those American novels written between the wars by means of "the objective method," or, in other words, relying on "what we might have seen or heard ourselves if we had been present at the scene."[8] She explained the effect these novels had had on world literature, largely because of the wide range of characters that can be empathetically portrayed in this objective style:

> French novels of the period between 1914 and 1932 give only a very biased picture of the country, a picture of only the most fortunate of its middle class. The American novel blew a fresh wind into the Republic of Letters. It also had the charm of exoticism—not in the banal sense of something geographically remote but in the more profound sense of social unfamiliarity. It portrays vagabonds, inveterate drunkards, the unemployed; tough guys stripped of all romanticism—simple victims of economic misfortune, caught in the determinism of an inflexible social structure; black people separated from white people by barriers even more insuperable than those of poverty; men who do not know how to read or write and who can barely speak well enough to express their most basic needs. All of them, however, are endowed with an incontestable human reality; all of them, in Christian terms, "have a soul." Because of this, the American novel restores to us, almost unintentionally, a certain idea of *man*, independent of the accidents of class and conditions. Truly classic in spirit—classic in the same ways as Chaplin's movies, which make people laugh in Shanghai as well as in Romorantin—it is more nearly universal than our eighteenth-century literature because it truly encompasses all races and all classes. It is coextensive with the planet. It demonstrates the principle of a new humanism.[9]

The same year Magny wrote this tribute, André Bazin, the influential French film critic, wrote with equal enthusiasm about the advent of the "objective" American novel[10]: it is "the most important literary revolution of our time."[11] He claimed that the Italian neo-realism movement in film—particularly the work of Roberto Rossellini—amounted to "simply the equivalent on film of the American novel."[12] "It is in Italy, naturally and with an ease that excludes any notion of deliberate and willful imitation, that the cinema of American literature has become a reality."[13]

This "literary revolution" can open the door for you as a writer. Film novels are not only a great way to tell a story, they are a great way to get into the film industry. Instead of writing a script and hoping it will get filmed, you can write and publish a film novel. Then you can submit a script version of the novel to film producers looking for novels to film (there are many such producers).

Let's now look at some examples of film novels and the films based on them. As we do, we will identify the literary devices they use, and we will evaluate how well they engage readers. It is important for you to start evaluating the film novels you read, thinking about their good and bad qualities. That will prepare you for the discussion in the next chapter about what makes film novels excellent.

## Hammett

The first film novel, *The Maltese Falcon*, was published in the United States in 1930 by Dashiell Hammett. This short detective novel consists of one visual scene after another, so that reading it is like watching a movie in your head.[14] It uses almost all dialogue and scene description, with no narration or interior monologue.[15] It is linear—with no flashbacks, flash-forwards, or imagined scenes.[16] Formally, then, it would be identified as a simple film novel.

The novel opens with a description of detective Samuel Spade:

**Dashiell Hammet**

Samuel Spade's jaw was long and bony, his chin a jutting v under the more flexible v of his mouth. His nostrils curved back to make another, smaller, v. His yellow-grey eyes were horizontal. The v *motif* was picked up again by thickish brows rising outward from twin creases above a hooked nose, and his pale brown hair grew down—from high flat temples—in a point on his forehead. He looked rather pleasantly like a blond satan.

He said to Effie Perine: "Yes, sweetheart?"

She was a lanky, sunburned girl whose tan dress of thin woolen stuff clung to her with an effect of dampness. Her eyes were brown and playful in a shiny boyish face. She finished shutting the door behind her, leaned against it, and said: "There's a girl wants to see you. Her name's Wonderly."

"A customer?"

"I guess so. You'll want to see her anyway: she's a knockout."
"Shoo her in, darling," said Spade. "Shoo her in."[17]

*The Maltese Falcon* is written in what Magny calls a "strict application of the objective method."[18] Its style is "admirably sparse and austere."[19] It is written with "restraint" and "circumspection."[20] These characteristics, Magny explains, enable Hammett to create "ambiguous" and surprising characters. In other words, by means of the style, "Hammett is able to endow his characters' intentions and secret desires" with "ambiguity," "thus surprising us as much as the actors in his dramas by unforeseeable actions and abrupt changes of circumstance."[21] As a result, we are invited to interpret the thoughts and feelings and attitudes of the characters, which are "more than the sum of [their] acts."[22] The characters stand out from their actions, without the author having "to pile on adventitious details," like "superficial mannerisms," or "a Herculean strength, a morbid passion for chamber music, cocaine, or French cooking."[23] As Magny puts it, "There is no danger that these heroes will be absorbed into the confusion of events; their personalities will always emerge from the plot, no matter how complex it may be."[24] In short, by using just dialogue and scene description, Hammett creates engaging characters that are not at all predictable or superficial.

Because *The Maltese Falcon* was a film novel, John Huston was able to film it in the specific ways that Hammett wrote it. Huston explains that the novel is "told entirely from the standpoint of Sam Spade, and so too, is the picture, with Spade in every scene except the murder of his partner."[25] (The murder scene was added to the film—it wasn't in the novel.) "All the

The Maltese Falcon, 1941

other characters are introduced only as they meet Spade," and they are photographed "through his eyes."[26] This focus on Spade's point of view in the film and the novel draws the reader into the action. And it was the point of view technique in the novel that led the way to the technique in the film. At the time, point-of-view filming was, as Huston put it, "something of an innovation."[27] But, he explains, "since then, the camera as [the] protagonist has become a familiar technique."[28]

## Faulkner

Meanwhile, in 1931, William Faulkner published *Sanctuary*. It is a narrated film novel with flashbacks—a complex film novel. But *Sanctuary* is less complex than Faulkner's earlier novels, like *The Sound and the Fury*, which is more like *Ulysses*.[29] Faulkner had a great deal of respect for *Ulysses*: "You should approach Joyce's *Ulysses*," he told a *Paris Review* interviewer, "as the illiterate Baptist preacher approaches the Old Testament: with faith."[30] In *Sanctuary*, Faulkner uses the narrative techniques of *Ulysses*, but sparingly.

**William Faulkner**

Sanctuary was Faulkner's first best seller. Some critics consider it one of his most enigmatic and influential novels.[31] It begins simply, like *Ulysses,* with dialogue and scene description, first from one character's point of view and then from another's:

> From beyond the screen of bushes which surrounded the spring, Popeye watched the man drinking. A faint path led from the road to the spring. Popeye watched the man—a tall, thin man, hatless, in worn gray flannel trousers and carrying a tweed coat over his arm—emerge from the path and kneel to drink from the spring.
>
> The spring welled up at the root of a beech tree and flowed away upon a bottom of whorled and waved sand. It was surrounded by a thick growth of cane and brier, of cypress and gum in which broken sunlight lay sourceless. Somewhere, hidden and secret yet nearby, a bird sang three notes and ceased.
>
> In the spring the drinking man leaned his face to the broken and myriad reflection of his own drinking. When he rose up he saw among them the shattered reflection of Popeye's straw hat, though he had heard no sound.[32]

Later in the novel, we find narration that can be used as voice-over in scenes. The following passage is an example:

> On the next afternoon Benbow was at his sister's home. It was in the country, four miles from Jefferson; the home of her husband's people. She was a widow, with a boy ten years old, living in a big house with her son and the great aunt of her husband; a woman of ninety, who lived in a wheel chair, who was known as Miss Jenny. She and Benbow were at the window, watching his sister and a young man walking in the garden. His sister had been a widow for ten years.
>
> "Why hasn't she ever married again?" Benbow said.
>
> "I ask you," Miss Jenny said. "A young woman needs a man."
>
> "But not that one," Benbow said. The man wore flannels and a blue coat; a broad, plump young man with a swaggering air, vaguely collegiate. "She seems to like children. Maybe because she has one of her own now. Which one is that? Is that the same one she had last fall?"
>
> "Gowan Stevens," Miss Jenny said. "You ought to remember Gowan."
>
> "Yes," Benbow said. "I do now. I remember last October."[33]

We could rewrite the passage in script format like this, with first-person voice-over narration:

INT. HOUSE—DAY

Benbow and Miss Jenny are at the window.

                    BENBOW (V.O.)
          On the next afternoon, I was
          at my sister's home. It was in
          the country, four miles from
          Jefferson; the home of her hus-
          band's people. She was a widow,
          with a boy ten years old, liv-
          ing in a big house with her son
          and the great aunt of her hus-
          band; a woman of ninety, who
          lived in a wheel chair, who was
          known as Miss Jenny.

They watch his sister and a young man walking in
the garden.

                    BENBOW (V.O.)
          My sister had been a widow for
          ten years.

                    BENBOW
          Why hasn't she ever married
          again?

                    MISS JENNY
          I ask you. A young woman needs
          a man.

                    BENBOW
          But not that one.

The man wears flannels and a blue coat; a broad,
plump young man with a swaggering air, vaguely
collegiate.

                    BENBOW
          She seems to like children.
          Maybe because she has one of
          her own now. Which one is that?
          Is that the same one she had
          last fall?

>                     MISS JENNY
>     Gowan   Stevens.   You   ought   to
>     remember Gowan.
>
>                      BENBOW
>     Yes. I do now. I remember last
>     October.

In the last chapter of the novel, Faulkner uses narration, not only to show us the past, but to move quickly through the present. The last chapter is complex but easy to visualize.

Most of *Sanctuary* is easy to visualize, but the characters are often difficult, if not impossible, to understand. An explanation for this obscurity—given by both Sartre and Magny—is that Faulkner's characters act for reasons existing in the distant past, rather than in the immediate scene. Magny explains:

> [Faulkner] is sure that a person's true reality does not reside, as common sense would have it, in the actions he is completing or the feeling he is experiencing *now*, but that it is completely situated in the past, whether it is his own past or that of his race…. Because the characters in his stories regard the past so persistently, they allow themselves to be bewitched and devoured by it; it sometimes seems as if they willingly give it permission to overwhelm them.[34]

Magny explains that Sartre "[protested] against such alienation of man from his freedom."[35] (The next chapter explores Sartre's ideas about freedom.) Other critics object to the trapped nature of the characters in *Sanctuary*. One critic calls it a "wretched novel."[36]

Magny also claims that Faulkner was "deliberately obscure."[37] Sartre calls him a magician with a trick: "The trick lies in not telling, in keeping secrets—surreptitiously."[38] Faulkner might tell us that someone is upset, Sartre explains, but rapidly, in "a half-phrase that might almost pass unnoticed" if we aren't paying close attention.[39] Then when we "[expect] stormy outbreaks," he gives us "a minute and lengthy description of … gestures," with "no descriptive purpose,"[40] except to keep us guessing. He does this, Sartre writes, because "whatever is touched by divination becomes magical,"[41] meaning that as long as Faulkner keeps us searching for clues to hidden thoughts and feelings, his characters seem wonderful to us. But, as Magny writes, the reader is "tempted to cry mercy" and protest "against the uncustomary effort expected of him by accusing the author of being arbitrary and even perverse."[42] So, while Hammett encourages interpretation with his subtlety, Faulkner frustrates it with his ambiguity.

*Sanctuary* was twice adapted to film (first in 1933 as *The Story of Temple Drake* and then in l960 as *Sanctuary*), both times, as one critic claims, deplorably.[43] Both films cut out Popeye, a main character of the novel.[44] A year after the publication of *Sanctuary*, Faulkner published his next novel, *Light in August*. Interestingly enough, Carl Dreyer considered filming it, but never did.[45]

## Steinbeck

In l936 John Steinbeck wrote *In Dubious Battle*, a film novel about a violent agricultural strike in California. It is a simple novel, with almost no narration or

**John Steinbeck**

interior monologue. Steinbeck writes that he "had planned to write a journalistic account of a strike."[46] But his agent suggested he make it a piece of fiction. Steinbeck writes, "As I thought of it as fiction the thing got bigger and bigger."[47] He explains how he wrote it—he was "merely a recording consciousness, judging nothing, simply putting down the thing."[48] The novel opens with just scene description:

At last it was evening. The lights in the street outside came on, and the Neon [*sic*] restaurant sign on the corner jerked on and off, exploding its hard red light in the air. Into Jim Nolan's room the sign threw a soft red light. For two hours Jim had been sitting in a small, hard rocking-chair, his feet up on the white bedspread. Now that it was quite dark, he brought his feet down to the floor and slapped the sleeping legs. For a moment he sat quietly while waves of itching rolled up and down his calves; then he stood up and reached for the unshaded light. The furnished room lighted up—the big white bed with its chalk-white spread, the golden-oak bureau, the clean red carpet worn through to a brown warp.

Jim stepped to the washstand in the corner and washed his hands and combed water through his hair with his fingers. Looking into the mirror fastened across the corner of the room above the washstand, he peered into his own small grey eyes for a moment. From an inside pocket he took a comb fitted with a pocket clip and combed his straight brown hair, and parted it neatly on the side.[49]

His first artistically significant novel, *In Dubious Battle* moved Steinbeck into his major period of writing. A year later, he published a second film novel, *Of Mice and Men*, and two years after that, *The Grapes of Wrath*, in which every other chapter is written like a film novel. *Of Mice and Men* was filmed two years after it was written. The director was Lewis Milestone, who,

**Jean-Paul Sartre**

like John Huston, thrived on directing adaptations of novels. *Of Mice and Men* was again filmed in 1970 (for television), again in 1982, and then again in 1992 (for theatrical release). In 1950 Steinbeck wrote a third film novel, *Burning Bright*. This novel became a play but not a film.[50] Both *Of Mice and Men* and *Burning Bright* are essentially unnarrated film novels. In the preface to *Burning Bright*, Steinbeck calls both of these novels (as well *The Moon Is Down*, which he wrote between the two previous novels) easy-to-read scripts or short novels that can be performed—without the usual revisions made to novels—by simply lifting out the dialogue.[51] He also explains that his scene descriptions can help directors set up and film the scenes.

Steinbeck, as Magny explains, was one of the American writers who helped enlarge the realm of characters considered suitable for literature. Because of his "objectivity of vision," he was able to put onstage "characters of the lowest social class, like those in ... *In Dubious Battle* [and] retarded people like Lennie in *Of Mice and Men*."[52] At the same time, he was able to portray his characters sympathetically. He was striving for what he calls an "understanding-acceptance" of his characters.[53] Steinbeck explains that from acceptance of characters emerges a moral understanding, beyond "traditional or personal" standards of how characters "should be, or could be, or might be."[54] For example, he shows us the endearing qualities of Lennie, which invite us to accept him, before he asks us to morally assess this man "who strangles mice and women though he only wants to caress them."[55]

## Sartre

While Steinbeck was writing film novels in America, the French began writing them also. They called them *cinema novels*. In 1946 novelist, playwright, and philosopher Jean-Paul Sartre wrote *Les Jeux Sont Faits* (in English, *The Chips Are Down*), which is considered one of the earliest cinema novels.[56] Filmed a year after it was written, the story is told with just dialogue and scene description in 72 titled scenes, some of which are montage sequences of short scenes. "What makes the written narrative [of Sartre's novel] most similar to a film," film critic Bruce Morrissette writes, "is the rhythm of the ... scene cutting, especially in the sequences of increasingly rapid alternating scenes of decreasing duration depicting the parallel stories of the hero and heroine at the beginning."[57] As this critic observes, the novel isn't written from the point of view of the characters, despite Sartre's "theoretical pronouncement" that after Einstein, "the only logical or acceptable point of view must be a relative one anchored in the consciousness of an individual observer."[58] Because the novel isn't written from the point of view of the characters, it engages us less intimately in understanding it.

The novel opens with a scene of a man putting something in the water glass of his sleeping wife. The description begins by tracking a ray of light from the window:

> A room in which the half closed shutters let in only a streak of light. A ray falls on a woman's hand whose contracted fingers claw at the fur coverlet. The light shines on a gold wedding-ring, then, gliding up the arm, falls on the face of Eve Charlier ... With closed eyes and pinched nostrils, she seems to be in pain, tosses, groans.
>
> A door opens and in the opening a man pauses. Elegantly dressed, very dark with beautiful brown eyes, an American-style moustache, he seems to be thirty-five or thereabouts. It is André Charlier.

He looks intently at his wife, but with a cold scrutiny entirely devoid of tenderness.

He enters, closes the door noiselessly, tiptoes across the room, and stands looking down at Eve who has not heard him come in.

Lying on the bed, she is dressed in a very elegant dressing gown over her night dress. A fur coverlet is thrown over her legs.

For an instant André Charlier contemplates his wife, whose face shows intense suffering; then he bends down calling softly:

"Eve … Eve …"

Eve does not open her eyes. Her face contorted with pain, Eve sleeps.

André straightens up, turns his head toward the bedside-table where a glass of water is standing. He takes a bottle with a medicine-dropper out of his pocket and presses a few drops into the glass.

But, as Eve moves her head on the pillow, he hastily puts the bottle back in his pocket and gives his sleeping wife a sharp, hard glance.[59]

The woman dies and goes to heaven, where she meets the soul mate she was supposed to have found on earth. She and he are allowed to return and stay if, within a specified period, they can show complete confidence in each other. The theme of confidence, running through the novel, engages

The Misfits, 1961

us philosophically and psychologically. We ask, "What is confidence?" and "Are the characters confident in each other now?" We are engaged in trying to understand a concept and in trying to interpret characters in the light of that concept.

## Miller

In 1957 playwright Arthur Miller wrote *The Misfits*. He called it "a story conceived as a film";[60] he also called it a cinema novel.[61] The novel is written in present tense and uses speech tags much like those in scripts:

> At a certain point Main Street becomes a bridge crossing the narrow Truckee River, which flows between buildings. Roslyn and Isabelle are walking along, but Isabelle stops her at the railing. The heat of noon seems to have wilted them.
> Isabelle: "If you throw your ring in you'll never have a divorce again."
> Puzzled, Roslyn touches her ring protectively.
> Isabelle: "Go ahead, honey, everybody does it. There's more gold in that river than the Klondike."
> Roslyn, with a certain revulsion: "Did you do it?"
> Isabelle: "Me? Oh, I lost my ring on my honeymoon!"
> Roslyn: "Let's get a drink."
> Isabelle: "That's my girl!"[62]

"Movies, the most widespread form of art on earth," Miller explains in the preface, "have willy-nilly created a particular way of seeing life."[63] Movies, with "their swift transitions, their sudden bringing together of disparate images, their effect of documentation inevitable in photography, their economy of storytelling, and their concentration on mute action have infiltrated the novel and play writing—especially the latter—without being confessed to or, at times, being consciously realized at all."[64] The cinema novel, Miller writes, takes up these "vigorous" filmic ways of viewing life.[65] In short, film novels read like movies in our heads.

Miller also explains how he wrote *The Misfits*: with an economy of storytelling, every word either telling actors what to say (dialogue) or the camera what to see (scene description). Still, he wrote a number of passages that use narration—for example, ones in which new characters are introduced.

Miller engages his readers' empathy by writing from the point of view of his characters. He often changes the point-of-view character from one scene to the next, sometimes in the middle of scenes. Here is an example that begins with the point of view of Gay and then shifts to that of Roslyn and Guido:

> [Gay] turns and climbs up onto the hood of the car; he is very drunk, and shaken. He looks over the crowded street from this new elevation. Just below him Roslyn and Guido are looking up into his face, and he seems twice his normal size.[66]

Miller is often explicit, rather than implicit, about what his characters are thinking, feeling, and intending:

> There is a rural pathos in her eyes, an uprooted quality in the intense mistrust with which she walks.[67]

Here is another example:

> She is afraid she has been a fool and is trying to find out by searching Gay's eyes; she wears a joyless smile that is full of fear and unhappiness.[68]

Sometimes his descriptions of thoughts and feelings are vague or uncertain:

> He is strangely embarrassed and ashamed of his own shyness.[69]

> Now he seems either content or exhausted.[70]

The fact that he often tells us what to think of his characters engages us, in a certain way, in picturing his scenes; given his conclusions about characters, we imagine the evidence—we imagine what the scene must look like in order for him to draw his conclusions. (The more established approach is to describe characters in detail so that readers can infer what they are thinking, feeling, or trying to do—a major topic in the next chapter.)

The Misfits was filmed in 1961. The director was John Huston, filming his second film novel. But this time, he significantly departed from the novel. Miller's "original story," as one critic puts it, "celebrates a kind of archaic but good-natured machismo," with "cowpokes competing for [a] Reno divorcée."[71] But Marilyn Monroe (cast as the divorcée) "hated her sex goddess image," and Clark Gable (cast as the main cowpoke) couldn't seem to "allow himself to play the character Miller had in mind." So the parts for Monroe and Gable were rewritten "well past the last day of shooting."[72]

Huston and Miller frequently argued about whether or not a scene should be shot from the perspective of a character. Miller thought "a key scene should be seen from a main character's perspective," but Huston thought it should be seen "in a neutral omniscient manner."[73] The point-of-view scene mentioned earlier, the one about the drunk on the car, was shot from neither Gay's point of view looking down, nor Roslyn's and Guido's looking up. "The suggestions of alternating point of view in the published version of *The Misfits* are not carried out in the film itself."[74] Even though Huston felt comfortable preserving the point of view of the central character in *The Maltese Falcon,* he apparently didn't feel comfortable preserving the multiple points of view of the characters in *The Misfits.* Because the film isn't shot from the point of view of characters, it engages its viewers less intimately in their action than it otherwise might. Huston needed to learn how films, like novels, can shift point of view, a topic we come to in the last chapter.

## Going Beyond

Most of the film novels we have looked at in this chapter have been simple ones: (1) they use dialogue, scene description, and montages of scenes; (2) they don't use flashbacks, flash-forwards, or imagined scenes; and (3) they don't use narration or interior monologue. Most American film novels have been simple ones. But there are good reasons for film novelists to be open to the possibility of writing their film novels with greater complexity.

First, more complex film novels have flourished in France, which arguably has the richest film culture in the world—on an average weekend there

**Shawshank Redemption, 1994**

are over 300 films showing in Paris. After Magny, Bazin, and Sartre championed the film novel genre in France, a new generation of film novelists emerged there, including Alain Robbe-Grillet, Nathalie Sarraute, Michel Butor, and Claude Simon. One theorist explains how Alain Robbe-Gillet included all the aural and visual elements of a script in his film novel:

> Robbe-Grillet had furnished a script [for the film *Marienbad*] so complete in every detail of dialogue and visual images that it could have been turned over to an "electronic robot" for the actual filming. The original script was typed (as was customary at the time) on facing pages, one containing the dialogue and sound effects, the other the visual angles, lighting, actors' movement, and the like. To compose the printed cinema novel, Robbe-Grillet took the two sets of pages, sound and images, and melded them much as one might shuffle a deck of cards.[75]

To Americans, French film novels often seem overly complex, as do the films based on them, and to lack strong plots. But these are not insurmountable problems. In upcoming chapters, you will learn how to write film novels that preserve the American desire for strong plots. You will also learn how to judiciously use the complex elements that the French appreciate.

Second, many good films use flashbacks, imagined scenes, and voice-over for narration or interior monologue. Think, for example, of the flashbacks in *Forrest Gump*: most of the film is Forrest remembering his past. *Dumb and Dumber* uses imagined scenes well: for example, when the lead character encounters the husband of his love interest, in his imagination he pulls out a gun and shoots the husband. Flashbacks and imagined scenes can convey the subjective thoughts and wishes of a character, and they can convey the narrator's view of what really happened in the past or could yet happen in the future.

Voice-over for narration or interior monologue works more effectively in films than we might think. (See Sarah Kozloff's *Invisible Storytellers* for a long list of films that use voice-over well.) Think of the interior monologue of the boy in *A Christmas Story*, which conveys his anxiety about whether or not he will ever get a BB gun. Or think of the narration in Frank Darabont's *The Shawshank Redemption*, a script based on a story by Stephen King. (You can read the complete script at www.script-o-rama.com.) This script could easily be written as a film novel using a first-person, past-tense voice.

Third, some contemporary short fiction uses narration and interior monologue in effective ways that film novels could use. Consider, for example, the narration in a story by Tobias Wolff, which gives us additional evidence to use in assessing character. Notice how the narration comes during pauses in the action, so that it doesn't slow the scene down. (I have italicized the narration, which in a film would likely be read in first person.)

They were doing the dishes, his wife washing while he dried. *He'd washed the night before. Unlike most men he knew, he really pitched in on the housework. A few months earlier he'd overheard a friend of his wife's congratulate her on having such a considerate husband, and he thought, I try. Helping out with the dishes was a way he had of showing how considerate he was.*

*They talked about different things and somehow got on the subject of whether white people should marry black people.* He said that all things considered, he thought it was a bad idea.

"Why?" she asked.

*Sometimes his wife got this look where she pinched her brows together and bit her lower lip and stared down at something. When he saw her like this he knew he should keep his mouth shut, but he never did. Actually it made him talk more. She had that look now.*[76]

The scene could easily be included in a film novel.

Or consider the use of interior monologue in a story by Jayne Anne Phillips. She uses interior monologue (which in a film would be spoken in present tense and first person) for Jancy's observations in the present:

The meat sizzled on Jancy's plate and she tried to eat. She looked up. *The lines in her mother's face seemed deeper than before, grown in. And she was so thin, so perfectly groomed. Earrings. Creased pants. Silk scarves.*[77]

She also uses interior monologue for Jancy's imagining of the future:

Jancy wore a skirt and sat in the living room. *Her father would pull up outside. She would see him lean to watch the door of the house, his head inclined toward her. His car shining and just washed. His hat. His cigar. His baggy pants bought at the same store downtown for thirty years.*[78]

Again, scenes like these could be included in a film novel.

Narration and interior monologue can be powerful in a film novel. But it is difficult to use them. In a film script, we can use one voice to narrate and another to describe scenes; but in a film novel, we need to use the same voice for both narration and description. Still, to write a film novel without narration or interior monologue—to restrict ourselves to just dialogue and description of scenes—is also difficult. It may not only be easier but more engaging to use narration judiciously, as do Joyce and Faulkner and the biblical writers.

The Bible shows us its characters' actions mostly from their point of view, but now and then the narrator prompts us to reflect on those actions so that we can come to a shared understanding with the narrator and some of the characters. The Bible may still be our most reliable model of storytelling. It encapsulates so many of the best methods. In the chapters coming up, I will repeatedly refer to the way the Bible tells its stories, in part because the very writers who have written more filmically, like Faulconer and Steinbeck, were deeply influenced by biblical methods.

## Choosing a Subject to Write About

Now, where can you (yourself or with a group of writers, perhaps in a class) find ideas for writing a film novel? First of all, you can look for already-written scripts. If you find one, you will be able to write your film novel much faster, since you won't have to figure out everything from scratch. But you will need to remember that if you try to fix everything in a script, which is the tendency of many new writers, you will lose the benefit of starting with a script. You need to find what already works and try to preserve it. To find a script, do a Google search for Unproduced Screenplays. (There are thousands of them—for example at InkTip.com and HollywoodLitSales.com.) Find one you like, contact the author, offer to turn it into a novel (preserving the right to change what you need to), and work out an agreement on sharing proceeds from the publication and filming of the novel. Many writers of unproduced scripts will jump at the offer, particularly if their scripts have been unproduced for some time, and there are thousands of those too. Another option is to go to www.greatcinemanow.com/filmnovelist, which is a site I help maintain, where you will find a list of scripts that can be turned into film novels.

A second option is to find a novel or film you like—say in the bookstore or library—contact the owner of the copyright, and offer to write a film novel for it and, again, share the proceeds. Or you may find public-domain novels or films you like. You can rewrite one of these without having to contact anyone. (You can find out where to look for public-domain films and novels on Wikipedia.)

Third, you can go to people who have stories to tell. Find marriage counselors, policemen, judges, ex-senators, counselors at juvenile-correction centers—anyone who is likely to have good stories to tell about a subject you are interested in—and have them sign an agreement allowing you to tell their stories in novel form, perhaps for a share of the proceeds. Record their stories, and you may be able to make a film novel out of them. Or you may yourself have great stories to tell. Write them down, and you may be able to use them in making your film novel.

These are three main ways of finding something to write about, but it is important to remember that each of them is simply a way of getting background information. The actual work of writing your film novel will begin two chapters from now. The requirements are very specific, both in terms of the material you will need to come up with and how you will need to lay that material out. But finding subject material now, to draw from later, will be very helpful.

## The Next Chapter

So far, you have explored the formal elements of film novels—the dialogue, interior monologue, description, and narration that comprise them. You have seen how such writing has been used in past film novels, and you have considered how it might be used in future ones. But you haven't learned yet what it takes for a film novel to be well written. In the next chapter, drawing on the philosophy of Jean-Paul Sartre, you will explore in detail what it takes to write a film novel well.

## Student Writing Group

### Week Two

1. Read the introduction and assignments, and write your questions. Then read the chapter, and write your answers.

   *How are filmic literature and literary films made?* Filmic literature and literary films use elements that transcend both media. You create filmic literature by writing novels that can be visualized while being read, and you create literary films by experimenting with common literary elements, like shifting points of view, interior monologue, etc. (I have more questions and answers, but, alas, no space to put them here.)

2. Read a film novel suggested in the appendix, and copy down some scenes you like.

   I chose to read Anton Chekhov's novel *The Duel*. Here is an excerpt from one scene I quite liked.

   "The storm!" whispered Laevsky; he had a longing to pray to some one or to something, if only to the lightning or the storm-clouds. "Dear storm!"
   He remembered how as a boy he used to run out into the garden with-out a hat on when there was a storm, and how two fair-haired girls with

blue eyes used to run after him, and how they got wet through with the rain; they laughed with delight, but when there was a loud peal of thunder, the girls used to nestle up to the boy confidingly, while he crossed himself and made haste to repeat: "Holy, holy, holy…"

3. Now write a film novel scene yourself, using some of the sentences you wrote in the last chapter.

It was a typical morning in the community. While everyone else was working, Sam Sutter and his three buddies sat on the fort lookout, playing poker. Scattered around them were scraps of food—half-eaten sandwiches, small apples, and badly wrapped chocolates. The largest stash rested in front of Sam, who replaced his poker face with a wide grin. He set down a winning hand and laughed.

"It's been a pleasure boys." Sam pulled his winnings in while his friends complained loudly.

"You've got to be cheating," said Jake, frowning. Sam gave him a look of mock outrage.

"Where's the trust? Can't a guy just be born lucky?" he asked.

"Let's see how long luck lasts you out *there*," Nathan said, gesturing to outside their community. "Bet you wouldn't parade a royal flush in front of the rogueys."

Sam gave a short, derisive laugh. "What, *them*? Please. If I said 'three queens' they'd say, 'go fish.'"

All the boys started laughing. Their laughter was cut short when they heard Charlotte's voice.

"Sam?"

The boys reacted immediately. Dropping to their bellies, they lay still and stifled their laughter. Charlotte passed below them. She couldn't hear the laughter anymore. She knew her brother was hiding from her, but she also knew that there wasn't a thing she could do about it.

She called out once more before muttering to herself, "He never remembers."

The boys peeked down from the fort wall. The top of Charlotte's head was visible, but she didn't look up to see them. Eventually, she moved on.

The boys relaxed. Jake pumped his fist victoriously, but then turned and hit Sam lightly on the back of the head.

"You swiped my queen."

Sam gave Jake a sly smile. "She's too good for you." The other boys laughed, and Jake made a grab for Sam's cards

"Well, let's ask *her* what *she* thinks."

Sam was forced to stand up to keep his cards out of Jake's reach. As he chuckled, he took a quick glance at the dangerous lands outside the community. What he saw made him freeze. He dropped his cards and ran after Charlotte.

4. Find a story that you (as an individual or as a group, perhaps as a class) would like to turn into a screenplay and film novel. Or find a script you would like to rewrite and then turn into a film novel.

I am working on an assignment from Lyman Dayton, a producer I have worked with before. Lyman owns the story rights to a western film called *Against A Crooked Sky*, originally made in 1975. It made $20 million.

It has an awesome title and a powerful story, but Lyman agrees that Westerns are not what the industry is looking for. A large studio told him that it would be glad to help him bankroll several films—in the fantasy or sci-fi arena. So I proposed the preposterous: why not take the story out of its western setting and plop it into a postapocalyptic United States? The producer was intrigued. We gave it a shot.

So here we go. Grab your safety gear, and enter the future with me and Mel. We'll come back out, I promise.

# Subtext

In the last two chapters, you learned what film novels are—short novels of scene description interspersed in dialogue, interior monologue, or narration. In this chapter, you will learn what makes a good, well-written film novel: generosity. You will understand what generosity is in both reading and writing. You will realize how generous writing invites generous reading. You will understand how generosity is a key to moral assessment and comedy. And most importantly, you will understand how writing generously creates subtext. You will then practice writing generous scenes with subtext.

## Week Three

1. Read the introduction and assignments, and write your questions. Then read the chapter, and write your answers.
2. Copy down a scene you like from the stories or film novel you have been reading. Write subtext, in brackets, for the main characters in the scene and the narrator if there is one.
3. Write subtext, in brackets, for the main characters and the narrator if there is one, in the film novel scene you wrote in the last chapter or a revised version of it. Show a copy of your scene (without your added subtext) to one or two readers, and have them write, in brackets, *their* interpretations of the main characters and narrator. Insert their interpretations in the brackets with yours. Their interpretations and yours should be basically consistent with each other, but also somewhat different from each other. If they are not, you need to rewrite the scene.
4. Begin research for your story, taking notes about what you find.

*Glossary*

| | |
|---|---|
| **subtext** | What readers infer the characters and narrator are thinking, feeling, or trying to do |
| **generosity** | Coming to an empathetic understanding that others can empathetically come to |
| **well-written film novels** | Film novels that are written generously and so invite generous readings |
| **classical American philosophy** | Philosophies of Charles Peirce, William James, John Dewey, and Alfred North Whitehead, which emphasize how people and the universe develop through generous action |
| **tenderheartedness** | Generous action |
| **hard-heartedness** | Ungenerous action |

In 1944 Sartre launched a literary journal called *Les Temps Modernes*. It featured works in progress as well as reviews of published works.[1] In early issues of the journal, he developed, in effect, a philosophy for writing good film novels. He pulled together these reflections in his highly influential book *What Is Literature?* that he published in 1947, a year after the release of his own film novel *The Chips Are Down*.

In a 1999 interview, philosopher Jacques Derrida said that he had "learned a lot from Sartre's *What Is Literature?*" and that its questions—"What is the function of literature?" and "What does the writer do in society?"—were the questions he himself addressed "in almost [all of his] texts."[2] Sartre's basic claim is that when we write novels generously, we engage our readers in generously understanding us. What, according to Sartre, is generosity?

Shortly after exploring generous reading and writing in *What Is Literature?* Sartre wrote about the concept of generosity in several notebooks, which were published after his death as *Notebooks for an Ethics*. In this book he calls generosity a "value of action,"[3] and he links it with a type of Christian love: "Generosity. Love."[4] "God creates by an exuberant generosity."[5] Generosity is acting, not out of a need to get a certain response (God doesn't create out of need), but out of a love that invites love. Generosity is coming to an empathetic understanding that others can empathetically come to.

**Jacques Derrida**

The way to invite readers to empathetically understand our writing is to let them help us tell our story. Instead of telling it all ourselves, saying everything, we leave some things for our readers to infer. We let them infer subtext—what our characters and narrator are thinking, feeling, and trying to do. To understand how to write generously so that our readers can infer subtext, we first need to understand how to read generously. So we turn first to Sartre's views on generous reading and then to his views on generous writing.

## Generous Reading

In *What Is Literature?* Sartre discusses what it means to read generously. When we read generously, we create what Sartre calls a meaningful literary object. This means we give significance to words,[6] set up relationships between elements of a story,[7] and assess the thematic truths a story expresses.[8] Sartre describes how we help create the action of a story through "an imaginary participation in the action"[9:]

> In reading, one foresees; one waits. One foresees the end of the sentence, the following sentence, the next page. One waits for them to confirm or disappoint one's foresights. The reading is composed of a host of hypotheses, of dreams followed by awakenings, of hopes and deceptions.[10]

He also explains how we help create a character as we read: we attribute our "feelings" to "an imaginary personage" who embodies them for us and "who has no other substance than these borrowed passions."[11]

Along with the literary object, we also create a meaningful, sustaining universe. For example, when we create a literary object with a wheat field in it, we also create what supports the existence of that wheat field—the earth and human enterprise.[12] We make a meaningful "universe come into being."[13]

Of course, as readers we don't create the literary object and its sustaining universe out of nothing.[14] We are guided by the author:[15] we "recompose the beautiful object" from "the traces left by the artist."[16] "Reading is induction, interpolation, extrapolation" from what writers give us to work with in the text.[17] We are also guided by our backgrounds, our passions, presuppositions, sympathies, sexual temperaments, scales of values,[18] and also the world as it affects us.

Though we are influenced by the text, our past, and our environment, we still create our understanding freely. The creation of our understanding is "a new event"—one that cannot be explained by what already exists in the text, in our mind, or in the world.[19] It is "a continual exceeding of the written thing,"[20] a transformation "of the darkest masses of [our sensibilities],"[21] "a total renewal of the world."[22] Our understanding emerges, Sartre says, as an ab-solute beginning—meaning a beginning with no solution in what has been. "It is therefore brought about by the freedom of the reader."[23] Its creation is "a task proposed to human freedom" and so fills us with what Sartre calls joy.[24]

But when we deny our freedom and read ungenerously, we feel we must hold onto aspects of our past understanding, making sure those aspects are preserved in our new understanding. We experience a book as an ensemble of "obstacles and implements," thwarting or advancing aspects of ourselves we feel compelled to hold onto.[25] Because we won't let our presuppositions change, reading becomes "no longer anything but a means for feeding [our] hate or desire."[26] Instead of seeking out books that invite us to transform our thinking, we desire texts that align with our thoughts, and we hate those that don't.

When we read generously, we presume, until we have proven otherwise, that a book is the product of generosity. We give the author the benefit of the doubt by looking for a free creation, not one driven by stubbornly clung-to presuppositions. Presuming that the author is generous is being confident in the author, trusting the author, Sartre says.[27] Having confidence in each other, as we saw in the last chapter, is the theme of Sartre's film novel *The Chips Are Down*.

## Generous Writing

Following his discussion of generous reading, Sartre turns to generous writing. As we write generously, we continually reformulate our thinking about what we are writing. Our past thinking guides us but is transformed into new thinking. Generous writing, according to Sartre, "must not even be premeditated"—that is, it must not be determined by our past thinking or prior intentions.[28] In writing generously, our current agenda emerges in the moment of choice, guided by our past agenda. Our past agenda doesn't drive our current choice; it guides the choice of our renewed agenda. In other words, when we write generously, we leave our past experiences and our formed ideologies in the back of our mind and let our thinking emerge in the moment of writing. Writing generously isn't about conveying something we have decided on, so much as selectively drawing from previous thoughts in the moment of forming our present thoughts. In this way, nothing we do is premeditated—our past experiences have a passive influence, not a controlling one.

The generous writer, in Derrida's words, "is not a constituted subject that engages itself at a given moment in writing for some reason or another. [He] is *given* by writing ... born by being given."[29] Our own character, our self, with its beliefs and desires, emerges moment by moment as we write. That is, in each moment, what we do and believe and desire emerges freely, in response to what we and others have previously done and believed and desired.

"Certainly I do not deny ... that the author may be impassioned," Sartre writes. A writer can feel strongly about things. A writer can want to persuade others. But the generous writer "has transformed his emotions" into "free emotions," which are created "in an attitude of generosity."[30] Free emotions emerge, without bias, in response to what we and others have felt and thought. They emerge in the moment of creation, not beforehand as the cause of creation.

As generous writers, we appeal to the freedom and generosity of our future readers. We trust to their generosity the job of carrying out what we have begun;[31] we offer our writing as a task to their generosity;[32] we set up landmarks for our readers, but "the landmarks [we set] up are separated by the void. The reader must unite them; he must go beyond them."[33] In no case do we appeal to our reader's passivity. We don't "try to *affect* him, to communicate to him, from the very first, emotions of fear, desire, or anger" or a pat interpretation.[34] That would be, as Sartre puts it, to flatter our readers, to try to give them an understanding of the text obtainable without their generosity.

While a bad novel flatters, a good one is "an exigence and an act of faith," "an exigence and a gift." It is an exigence because it is a demand, a call, an invitation to our readers to be generous; it is an act of faith and a gift because it is a bestowal of confidence and trust in our readers that they will be generous.[35] In writing a generous novel, we assume our readers will interpret it in ways we can learn from. Derrida explains that, in writing, "you hope ... to discover or invent others who do not yet exist, but who nevertheless know something about [your topic] already, know more about it than you do."[36]

A generous novel, Sartre explains, can't be "gloomy," eliciting despair and a feeling of powerlessness, "since, however dark may be the colors in which one paints the world, one paints it only so that free men may feel their freedom as they face it."[37] With that sense of freedom, our readers may rise up to "the highest degree," even those who have "spent their lives hiding their freedom from themselves." "People who are known for their toughness," for example, may read a generous novel and be deeply moved "at the recital of imaginary misfortunes."[38]

In Sartre's view, when we write generously, we call others to act generously. The exercise of our generosity is thus an ethical demand that others also act generously. For "although literature is one thing and morality a quite different one, at the heart of the aesthetic imperative we discern the moral imperative."[39] Both literature and morality call us to treat others lovingly, generously, and without bias.

As a result of these ideas about generously reading and writing, Sartre played the role of "catalyst and mentor" to a new wave of French novelists (who often also made films) in the 1950s.[40] Robbe-Gillet, for example, "openly followed Sartre's lead by soliciting the reader's participation in actively 'inventing' the novel along with the author in a combined creative endeavor"—leaving his readers to figure out, for example, when his characters were seeing, remembering, or imagining scenes.[41] French novelists, and by extension filmmakers, found themselves "obliged ... to induce the reader to participate more actively."[42]

So far in this chapter, we have considered Sartre's ideas about reading and writing generously. We have seen that generosity is a means of freely coming to a new understanding and inviting others to do so as well. We can better understand how generosity keeps us connected to our past selves, to others, and to our environment, by considering classical American philosophy, which articulates ideas about sympathy, love, and tenderness that are similar to Sartre's ideas about generosity. These views, we will find, are closely allied with moral thought.

## Generosity and American Philosophy

Classical American philosophy was formulated by Charles Peirce (considered its father), William James (who called it pragmatism), John Dewey (who extended it into ethics and education), and Alfred North Whitehead (who extended it into quantum physics). For these thinkers, objects and people deterministically banging up against each other aren't the fundamental elements of the universe. Instead, the fundamental elements are events, which draw on the potentialities of past events. Objects, whether animate or inanimate, are simply connected sequences of events. Bertrand Russell writes, "It is obvious that our old comfortable notion of 'solid matter' cannot survive. A piece of matter is nothing but a series of events obeying certain laws."[43] So a particle isn't an entity moving through a space–time field; it is a sequence of fluctuations in the field. (For a physical demonstration of this idea, see "Dr. Quantum—Double Slit Experiment" on *YouTube,* which has been viewed over a million and a half times.) It is like the moving light on a marquee—a sequence of flashes. A person is a sequence of actions, each building on the potentialities of previous actions, including the actions of others nearby.

**Alfred North Whitehead**

**Bertrand Russell**

In other words, we are what we are because of what we do; we don't do what we do because of what we are. We are kind because we act kind; we don't act kind because we are kind. In Sartre's terms, existence proceeds essence. Biblical scholar Shimon Bar-Efrat uses these terms to describe characters in the Bible:

> In many biblical narratives a person's character is not regarded as constant, but as something continually shifting and changing, even though stable components can be discerned. Character is existential rather than essential, since it is revealed in actual and transient real-life situations.[44]

So instead of having essences that drive our actions, we are always re-creating who we are by the actions we perform. The same can be true of the characters we create: instead of being types—like the fearless Achilles or noble Hektor, or more contemporarily, the kind-hearted aunt, the prickly boss, or the dim-witted P.E. teacher—our characters can unexpectedly change in the situations in which they find themselves—like the Jack Nicholson character does in *As Good as it Gets*, actually paying his date a real compliment, or Mr. Cunningham in *To Kill a Mockingbird*, turning the mob away from the jail after Scout speaks kindly to him.

In each moment, we actualize potentialities drawn from what has just happened around us and what we have just done. And in each moment of actualizing these potentialities, we are reborn, created anew, not out of nothing, but out of the immediate past, which carries with it the comprehensive past. We are re-created in constant bursts out of the lively aspects of the past in the same way literary worlds are re-created moment by moment. As generous writers, we let our past guide our writing but not control it; we live in the same way, drawing from our past experiences but not controlled by them.

The difference between us and things isn't the difference between minds and bodies. Things like tables and chairs are what Charles Peirce calls deadened minds—they are freely re-creating themselves moment by moment in ways that can't be predicted on the quantum micro level but can be predicted on the macro level. We, on the other hand, have fully developed minds—we can't be predicted, even on the macro level—at least when we are at our best and aren't hardening ourselves into thing-like roles. The difference between us and things, then, is our level of creativity—not that things are bodies and we are bodies with minds.

When we are most human, we are synthesizing and enhancing the promising aspects of events happening around us moment by moment. So, for example, if we see a jogger trip and fall on the sidewalk, we don't immediately decide exactly what we need to do. Instead, our body reacts, almost as if we had fallen (neurologists call this a mirror response), then our eyes squint slightly to block out other things so we can see the fallen victim more closely, then we move to help him and think consciously about how he may be hurt. At the same time, we foster the response of others by our efforts. We invite them to go beyond what we have done—to draw on the potentialities of our actions. As we hurry to the injured jogger, people see us, and we become a part of the reservoir they draw from when they make their choice to join us in helping the jogger. Then their existence in our lives makes them a part of our own reservoir. In the end, we and the others who have joined us lift our runner off the ground.

Through generosity we are linked to others. We become, to a degree, one with them as we develop the potentialities of what they have done. But this oneness isn't fixed; it must be continually renewed. We develop ideas, Peirce explains, because of our sympathy and love for others and their ideas. "The infinite diversity of the universe, which we call chance, may bring ideas into proximity that are not associated in one general idea."[45] We then form a new idea, "a mental association" that pulls what it can from the diverse ideas.[46] We do this by "cherishing and tending" those different ideas "as [we] would the flowers in [our] garden." "Love, recognizing germs of loveliness in the hateful, gradually warms it into life, and makes it lovely."[47] "Growth comes only from love, from—I will not say self-*sacrifice*"[48]—but from "every individual merging his individuality in sympathy with his neighbors."[49]

With this conception of love comes a new conception of God. In the classical tradition of American philosophy, God is neither the whole of being nor what lies behind the whole. He is neither the fixed reality behind the flux nor the order behind the apparent chaos. God is the supremely loving one, the one who comes to the most empathetic understanding that we can come to. He most fully synthesizes his understanding with ours so that we can synthesize our understanding with his. By drawing on his synthesis, we become linked to him and thereby more fully linked to others. He thus influences our understanding of others, not by force, but by what Whitehead calls "divine persuasion."[50] Through God, we become generously linked to a fundamentally pluralistic universe of persons. In such a universe, truth is scattered—there is always something to generously learn from others.

Not only can we be generously linked to God and other people, we can also be generously linked to the material world.[51] This link is possible, Whitehead explains, because mind and matter are fundamentally the same—both are events with dispositions and potentialities we can generously synthesize in our actions. When we accommodate ourselves to the material world, we generously adapt ourselves to the disposition of the matter around us and within us. We adapt our actions, moment by moment, to the physical momentum of, say, our feet and our hands, as well as the ground we stand on and the objects we touch. The more accommodating and generous we are in the physical world, the more graciously we act.

A person, Whitehead explains, is an "incorporated" society, "a society involving a vast number of [events], spatially and temporally coordinated."[52] When we speak, for example, we coordinate our delivery with changes of breath support and lip placement and a vast number of other events all coming together to provide a unity to our action. When we have generously unified the events that make up our actions, we have what Peirce and Whitehead call a personality. Similarly, when we have generously unified the writing of our novels and films, they have what filmmakers call a style and writers call a voice. Without this unity, we (and our creations) are uncoordinated, inept, and lacking in personality.

If our writing has a style, a voice, it is because we have generously written it in response to the world around us and within us. If a film novel like Steinbeck's *Of Mice and Men* has a voice that speaks for a generation of itinerant workers like George and Lennie, it is because Steinbeck has generously come to terms with that group of people and the world they faced. Generosity is the key to good writing. As we will see, it also provides the key to morally assessing characters.

## Generosity as Moral Action

When we generously come to a new attitude toward the world, John Dewey explains, we have acted morally, not because our new attitude agrees with some preexistent moral principle but because we have arrived at it morally—by seriously considering and drawing from other attitudes, preserving as much as possible of what is worthwhile in them.[53] Synthesizing diverse attitudes, such as alternatives in our own mind or the minds of others, is acting morally. Our attitudes cease to be moral when we cease to synthesize them, but instead replicate them, which makes us egotistical, insistent, and controlling.

A biblical term for Dewey's moral action is tenderheartedness, and one for its opposite is hardheartedness. A tender heart is impressionable, easily moved to love and pity; a hard heart is impenetrable, lacking in sympathetic responsiveness. Another biblical phrase for hardheartedness is stiff-neckedness, the neck being what we normally use to turn towards each other. In 2 Chronicles we read, "He stiffened his neck, and hardened his heart."[54] A related phrase is hardening the face, the face being the most visibly responsive part of ourselves—"A wicked man hardeneth his face."[55]

To be tenderhearted is to generously stay connected to each other and to our past selves. To be hard-hearted is to try to disconnect. We (and our characters) can harden our hearts by demeaning or ignoring aspects of our own attitudes and exaggerating others. We might, for example, construe another's need as an extraordinary demand and reject a feeling we have had that we should help, or we might go ahead and help but act as if we were making some magnificent heroic effort. In either case, our new attitude becomes a rationale for what we have rejected or distorted, not a synthesis of what we have accepted. Similarly, we (and our characters) can harden our hearts by ceasing to take seriously the attitudes of others. We can see their attitudes as obstacles to be overcome, vehicles for accomplishing our purposes, or viewpoints simply not worth considering. When we do so, we don't draw from their attitudes, and so we don't create attitudes they can connect with. As a result, they can't give us something new we can then draw from. Our own attitudes thus become fossilized, not renewed. They become *thing*-like.

When we harden our hearts, we invite others to harden theirs. Treating others as enemies to be destroyed, objects to be used, or things to be ignored invites them to harden their hearts in return. On the other hand, when we respond tenderheartedly to others, drawing what we can from them, connecting with them so that they can connect with us, our syntheses invite them to soften their hearts: "A soft answer turneth away wrath";[56] "A soft tongue breaketh the bone."[57]

It is important to realize, however, that a soft answer needn't be a quiet one. It is simply a tender, genuine, connected one. When, at the end of *Sounder,* the Cicely Tyson character calls her husband to task for getting angry and bossy with their disobedient son, she yells. But she stays connected to her husband, explaining that their son doesn't want to go away to school because he doesn't want to leave his father. When, at the end of the film *Trip to Bountiful,* the husband finally steps forward and calls his squabbling wife and mother to task, he too yells, saying, in effect, "We can't treat each other like this—we have to live in peace." Both women turn and look at him, touched by his tenderness. It is the high point of the film.

**Sounder, 1972**

It is also important to realize that generously staying connected to others needn't mean continuing to talk to them or even to stay in their presence. When others harden their hearts, we (and our characters) can respond tenderly by grieving, as if they had died, which in a sense they have. This grief can lead us to withdraw from them—give them space, stop talking to them, physically leave them—and periodically "poke them" to see if life has returned.

The film *On the Waterfront* provides an example of grieving in response to hardness. Charlie (played by Rod Steiger) tries to convince his brother Terry (played by Marlon Brando) to work for the mob. But Terry doesn't know if he wants to. In a last ditch effort, Charlie pulls a gun on Terry. The director, Elia Kazan, wanted Terry to be frightened. But Brando wanted to take the scene another direction—he felt that Terry should respond with grief instead of fright. Kazan and Brando agreed to play the scene both ways and keep the best one. In Brando's version of the scene, Terry shakes his head and says, "Oh, Charlie, Charlie." Charlie lowers the gun and slumps back in his seat. His jaw drops, but words don't come to him. Kazan decided to use Brando's version of the scene—one of the most powerful and memorable scenes in film history.

For an illuminating study of the many ways characters can harden and soften their hearts, see C. Terry Warner's book *Bonds That Make Us Free*.

**On the Waterfront, 1954**

## Generosity and Comedy

Besides providing a key to morally assessing character, generosity is also a key to understanding comedy. Both generous and ungenerous characters can be funny. Ungenerous characters are funny when they are obstinately unresponsive to the potentialities of the situations they find themselves in. We laugh, for example, when Miss Daisy, who is no longer able to drive, refuses to let Hoke (who is hired by her son) drive her anywhere. Henri Bergson, a French philosopher who wrote about humor, writes that

**Driving Miss Daisy, 1989**

comic characters err through "obstinacy of mind or of disposition, through absent-mindedness, in short, through automatism." He characterizes this obstinacy as "a sort of rigidity which compels its victims to keep strictly to one path, to follow it straight along, to shut their ears and refuse to listen."[58] However, as Aristotle warns us, obstinate, ungenerous behavior can't be too hurtful or destructive or we won't find it funny to watch.[59] One way to keep obstinate behavior funny is to put strong characters around the humorous character—characters like Hoke, who aren't easily hurt.

Not only can ungenerous characters be funny, so can generous ones. A generous character is responsive to the potentialities of the situations in which he finds himself and can be amazingly inventive, like Charley Chaplin when he rigs up a baby feeder in *The Kid* or cooks his boot in *The Gold Rush*. We laugh when characters successfully deal with difficult situations in rather odd, unpredictable ways—for instance, when Hoke drives beside Miss Daisy as she walks to the store.

With these philosophical, moral, and dramatic aspects of generosity in mind, we can now move on to discussing subtext.

## Subtext

French filmmaker Jean Renoir (the son of painter Pierre-Auguste Renoir) once said that the secret of creating art is to have more to say than we *can* say. In a novel, this means understanding more about our characters than we are willing to say about them because we are generously hoping our readers will come to their own understanding. If we understand a lot but proceed with restraint, our dialogue, scene description, and narration provide subtext—implicit (instead of explicit) indications of what our characters and narrator are thinking, feeling, and trying to do. This subtext, which emerges because of our generosity, invites the generous interpretation of our readers.

**Jean Renoir**

In the following story excerpt, the student writer could have said more about what her characters were thinking, feeling, and trying to do, but she exercised restraint in her writing, restricting herself to just the dialogue and description pertinent to the scene so that her readers could help create the meaning of the story. Because she had more to say than she allowed herself to say explicitly, her dialogue and description invite her readers to read between the lines. We have put in brackets the writer's interpretations of her characters and narrator and also a reader's interpretations so that they can be compared. Notice that the writer and reader differ in their understanding of what is happening—but not wildly so.

Her mother revved the engine, then flipped the car into reverse and laid on the gas again. [*Something is on her mind. Maybe she's agitated. / She is somehow upset.*] The car flew back and so did Gina and her cereal, which nearly spilled, despite the towel. [*The narrator is particularly concerned about Gina. / The narrator has chosen Gina as the point-of-view character.*] [*The mother is impatient, inconsiderate. / They're going to be late.*] Gina sighed loudly, but didn't speak. [*She is bothered. / She is passive-aggressive.*]

"Are you sure you can get a ride from seminary to school?" her mother asked, pressing each of the easy-reach radio buttons sequentially from one easy-listening station to another. [*She's frazzled, needs something to calm her. / She seems nervous and not too concerned about Gina, more about her own ease.*]

"Well," Gina looked straight at the road ahead, "if Angie's there I can—and she's never missed a day of seminary yet." [*She's bothered that her mother asks the question. / She's not connecting with her mom.*]

"You know you don't have to be so rude to me. There's no law that says fifteen-year-old girls need to be to rude to their mothers." [*She doesn't try to find out what's bothering Gina. / Small explosion—she's on the defensive.*]

"Whatever." She hit the seek button twice to the alternative rock station and looked out her window. [*All the buttons are programmed for her mother. / She's "pushing her mother's buttons."*]

"What's your problem lately anyway? What in the world have I done to deserve this?" [*Extreme response. / She's asserting her rights.*]

"I don't know…" Gina said, staring at the fuzzy burgundy floor mat. She climbed out of the car. "I have jazz band after school. I'll get a ride home." She bent over to lift her backpack and scripture case from the floor and slammed the door. [*Not really paying attention to what her mother is saying. / More nonverbal complaining.*]

The responses are basically consistent, but diverse. That means the subtext is working well. When the responses are exactly the same, that means the characters are clichéd and the writer hasn't required a generous response from readers. When the responses are wildly different, that means the characters are obscure and the writer hasn't given readers enough to work with.

## Research

If you do research for your story, you will be more likely to have a rich, authentic, and believable story, and you will give yourself resources to draw from as you write. You will also likely end up with more to say than you can easily say in a film novel, and your readers will then be able to generously read between the lines of your story. There are several areas you should research.

First, research your setting. If you are writing about the past, what was the world like back then; or if you are writing about the future, what would it be like? Does your story take place on a Pacific island? That will require in-depth research on the history, customs, and geography of the island. Even if your story is set in a modern-city (perhaps even your own hometown) and you feel that you are already familiar enough with the setting to create an authentic atmosphere for your characters, it is still likely that there are many relevant topics you should research.

Second, research your characters. What are your characters' temperaments, their likes and dislikes? Do any of them have debilitating diseases or careers you are unfamiliar with? Do any of them have any gadgets or weaponry that are sophisticated or highly advanced? What are their day-to-day activities? What do they eat, wear, drive, read, and watch?

Third, research the world of your intended audience. If you are writing a story about a person who lives in a fantasy world, for example, and eventually comes back to the real world, research the fantasy worlds your intended audience lives in—like escapist novels and films and social networks with online friends who take the place of face-to-face ones. If you research the worlds of both your audience and your characters, elements of this research will end up in your story, and your audience will find itself resonating with your characters.

Where can you do this research? There are a number of places where you can begin: public libraries, university libraries, reputable sources on the Internet, experts in the field (doctors, actors, high school teachers, marines, scientists, fashion designers, professors of ancient religions, etc.). If you let librarians and experts know you are writing a novel for a film, you may be surprised how willing they are to help you with your research. You can also do "in the field" research, visiting places like those you will write about, even possibly living out some of the experiences you wish to write about—within reason, of course.

## The Next Chapter

Up to this point in the book, you have explored the history and practice of writing short, easy-to-visualize novels that implicitly convey subtext. In the next chapters, you will move beyond these warm-ups: you will write three summaries of your story—first, a pitch (a one-sentence summary), then a synopsis (a five- to six-page summary of the main scenes), and finally a scenario (a fifteen- to twenty-page summary of all the scenes). Writing these summaries will prepare you to write a generous script and novel.

## Student Writing Group

### Week Three

1. Read the introduction and assignments, and write your questions. Then read the chapter, and write your answers.

   *It seems generous, to me, to give my readers a plethora of writing. So does the instruction to write "generously" contradict that understanding of mine? As a "generous" writer, I wouldn't lord an agenda over my work. Rather, I would lightly draw from the potentialities around me and from my past experiences—leaving the main work of writing to be spontaneous. In this way, I might surprise myself with what I've created. If I write generously, then my characters will be open to a reader's interpretation rather than being cardboard responders to my agenda, and my work will be free of ungenerous, didactic plots.*

2. Copy down a scene you like from the stories or film novel you have been reading. Write subtext, in brackets, for the main characters in the scene and the narrator if there is one.

   Here is subtext for an excerpt from a scene in Chekhov's *The Duel*:

   "Now we understand," said Von Koren, coming from behind the table. "Mr. Laevsky wants to amuse himself with a duel before he goes away. I can give him that pleasure. Mr. Laevsky, I accept your challenge." [*Von Koren is delighted with the aggravating effect he has had on the situation.*]

"A challenge," said Laevsky in a low voice, going up to the zoologist and looking with hatred at his swarthy brow and curly hair. "A challenge? By all means! I hate you! I hate you!" [*He is losing all decorum and rationality.*]

"Delighted. Tomorrow morning early, near Kerbalay's. I leave all details to your taste. And now, clear out!" [*He is confident and condescending; he sees Laevsky as no threat whatsoever.*]

"I hate you," Laevsky said softly, breathing hard. "I have hated you a long while! A duel! Yes!" [*He has a Gollumesque ability to convince himself it is right to feel extreme emotions when riled.*]

"Get rid of him, Alexandr Daviditch, or else I'm going," said Von Koren. "He'll bite me." [*He has only the greatest disdain for Laevsky.*]

3. Write subtext, in brackets, for the main characters and narrator if there is one, in the film novel scene you wrote in the last chapter or a revised version of it. Show a copy of your scene (without your added subtext) to one or two readers, and have them write, in brackets, *their* interpretations of the main characters and narrator. Insert their interpretations in the brackets with yours. Their interpretations and yours should be basically consistent with each other, but also somewhat different from each other. If they are not, you need to rewrite the scene.

Here is the subtext for the scene. The first interpretations in the brackets are mine, and the second are Mel's. If there are any third ones, I blame my pet alien.

The community bustled with morning activity below the fort lookout where Sam Sutter and his three buddies hid to play poker. [*Sam and company are not the hard-working type. / This is going to be a story about a young person named Sam—an "ordinary" kid, as he is hiding to play cards with buddies.*] Scattered food and wrappers surrounded them— half-eaten sandwiches, candy, caramel popcorn. In the middle was a pile of motley items used as wagers. The largest stash rested in front of Sam, who soon replaced his poker face with a wide grin. [*He's had a really good winning streak, and it's not over. / The boys have been playing for a while already; Sam is unapologetically winning.*] He set down a winning hand.

"It's been a pleasure, boys." Sam dragged his winnings closer while his friends complained loudly. [*His friends are tired of him winning. / Sam wins so often that his buddies are tired of it.*] He held up his hands.

"Hey, you guys, try winning three times straight. It's harder than it looks!" he said. [*Sam isn't modest. / Sam isn't sympathetic.*]

"How do you do it?" asked Jake, pointing at Sam. "You're cheating, aren't you?"

Mike and Nathan murmured their concurrence. Sam gave them all a look of disdain.

"Where's the trust? Can't a guy just be born to win?" he asked. [*Sam seems sure his friends won't revolt. / Sam is cocky; he believes he can outsmart most people and that there's no real harm in doing so.*]

Mike snorted and shook his head. "Every game?"

Sam shrugged and held up his hands innocently. "Luck is on my side." [*Sam has no empathy so long as he's on top. / More evidence of Sam's shameless cockiness.*]

"Let's see how long luck lasts you out *there*," Nathan said, jerking his head toward the fences. "Bet you wouldn't parade a royal flush in front of the rogueys." [*The boys have heard stories of what's outside their community but haven't experienced it themselves. / There is danger beyond; we don't know what kind—safety is inside.*]

Sam gave a short, derisive laugh. "What, *them*? Please. If I said 'straight flush,' they'd say, 'You have plumbing?'" [*Sam is a little too confident, poking fun at danger. / Sam is naïve, or he at least wants his friends to believe he's fearless.*]

All the boys started laughing, though Nathan was the last to join in the fun. [*Nathan is slightly antagonistic toward Sam. / Nathan is the most mature and realistic among them.*] Their laughter was cut short when a young woman's voice called out from a short distance away.

"Sam?"

The boys looked at each other with wide eyes. Nathan looked towards the voice and then turned to look at Sam.

"It's your sister!" [*The boys are afraid of being caught. / The boys panic, thinking they are going to be caught and put to work.*]

The boys reacted immediately. Dropping to their bellies, they lay still and put their hands over their mouths to stifle their laughter. [*They are playful and a little irresponsible. / The boys don't want to be found; it's hysterical to be hiding so close to the person who is in pursuit.*]

Charlotte walked below the perch where the boys were hiding. She paused for a moment, looking about every which way with a frown of puzzlement.

"Sam?" she called again before muttering to herself, "Today of all days. He never remembers." [*Charlotte isn't pleased that Sam is ruining her plans but is too mature to be mean-spirited about it. / Sam is knowingly neglecting something important, and Charlotte seems to be benevolently giving him the benefit of the doubt for "forgetting."*]

The boys peeked down from their hiding place on the fort wall. The top of Charlotte's head was visible, but she didn't look up to see them. They withdrew, holding their hands tighter over their mouths as they did their best not to laugh.

Just then, a small, white, butterfly-like insect landed on top of Sam's head. The other boys had to contain their laughter before pointing at it. Sam didn't understand what they were trying to sign, so they uncovered their mouths and mouthed, "Bug!" Sam swiped the bug off of his head. Then he flicked it to the ground below. [*Sam will do anything to make his friends laugh, even risk being caught. / Sam is happy to be the entertainment.*] The boys peered over the edge and saw that Charlotte had gone.

The friends uncovered their mouths and laughed. Jake pumped his fist victoriously.

"That was close," Mike muttered, picking his cards back up again.

The boys agreed with him. Jake turned to Sam and hit him lightly on the back of the head.

"Sam, I saw you swipe my queen."

Sam gave Jake a sly smile. "She's too good for you." [*Sam isn't concerned that Jake will get seriously angry. / Sam is not above cheating—or above pushing his luck with his friends' goodwill.*]

While Mike and Nathan laughed at him, Jake made a swipe for Sam's cards, speaking loudly.

"Oh, yeah?" he said. "Well, let's ask *her* what *she* thinks."

Sam was forced to stand up to keep his cards out of Jake's reach. He chuckled as he glanced out into the distance towards the dangerous lands outside the community. What he saw made him sober immediately; he dropped his cards and ran after Charlotte. [*Sam sees something serious enough to make him drop the "I'm the man" charade. / Sam's mood instantly changes when he sees something—it may be scary, dangerous, whatever—but he gets serious fast.*]

4. Begin research for your story, taking notes about what you find.

I asked two people to help me with the research—Melanie Henderson and Jake Cutler. There were two main areas I needed to research: the setting of a postapocalyptic world and Aztec beliefs.

To get information on the postapocalyptic setting, my fellow researchers and I chatted several times with Rick Fowler, a researcher in that field. He enlightened us with theories of how civilization might end and how the apocalypse might come about politically, financially, and religiously.

Mr. Fowler also helped us envision what sorts of groups, communities, methods of transportation and communication might exist in a postapocalyptic setting. Speaking with him, we were able to get some footing in creating the setting of the story, as well as enough conspiracy theorizing for us to lose sleep over.

The second half of our research was accomplished by interviewing Brigham Young University humanities professor Allen Christenson. He kindly agreed to sit with us and explain a lot about ancient Azetc beliefs. We learned several key things, such as the nature of Aztec worship, how important symbolism was to the Aztecs, their basic theological tenets, how gender roles were defined, and how they justified human sacrifice. After speaking with him, we were actually able to fix some key plot holes. Armed with knowledge, we are ready to proceed!

# Stage Two: Summarizing

# Pitch

So far you have been warming up. Now you will actually begin writing your script and film novel. In this chapter, you will learn why it is good to summarize your story first and flesh it out second. And you will write several possible pitches for your story—one sentence statements of what the main character's main line of action is. Then you will audience test your pitches and pick one for the script and film novel you will write.

### Week Four

1. Read the introduction and assignments, and write your questions. Then read the chapter, and write your answers.
2. Find pitches online for two movies you like, and write them down. Bear in mind that the ones you find online aren't likely to be as informative as those you will learn to write in this chapter.
3. Write at least two pitches for the story you are writing.
4. Audience test your pitches to find out which of them is strongest. Email at least six people, write a paragraph summarizing your experience with your respondents, and explain how this feedback can help you.

### Glossary

**line of action**     An extended action that builds to a significant insight or choice

**characterization**    A summary of the attitudes, desires, and intents of a character

**pitch**    A one-sentence statement of the main character's main line of action, with an initial and final characterization of the main character in that line of action

**soft-focus**    Focusing mainly on one thing and peripherally on other things

By far the most influential book ever written on drama is *Poetics* by Aristotle. In this book, Aristotle writes about the value of "constructing one's plots and [then] working them out in language."[1] Why that order? Why write plots first and then fill them out? The obvious answer is so that the scenes fit together. But if we construct the plot first, and the scenes have to fit the plot, won't that hamper our ability to write the scenes creatively?

To answer that question, let's return to the idea of generous writing. When we write generously, we creatively synthesize the influences around us. In doing this, Sartre writes, we aren't "engaged in partial enterprises." What he means is that we don't hold back any part of ourselves, and everything around us can be drawn from. But this needn't mean that we impartially actualize the potentialities of everything affecting us. It means that we impartially let one thing after another influence us most. In each moment, we may develop the potential of some influences more than others. The next moment, we may develop other influences more. This is the generous impartiality of parents who remain aware of all of their children's needs but focus on those of one child after another. So in writing generously, everything and everybody about us can influence our work, but we can't impartially incorporate everything and everybody. The result would be chaotic. Instead, we focus on some things more than others at one time or another.

**Aristotle**

**Martin Heidegger**

Because we can choose our focus, we are "*free* in an originary sense," Martin Heidegger writes.[2] It is this freedom, he says, that makes us different from animals. We choose to focus on various influences, but animals are "taken by" them, "captivated" by them.[3] Think of a mailman coming to our door: we can decide to concentrate on him, but our barking dog is captivated by him; we may focus our attention on him or not, but the dog is riveted. In other words, we are human because we can freely pick what we let influence us most.

The key to understanding how we can write scenes creatively within the framework of a preexisting plot is the freedom we have to pick what influences us most in each moment. As writers planning to write scenes, we focus our attention on the structure of what we will write—the plot. But in actually writing the scenes, we focus our attention on the details of the emerging scenes. Peripherally, we are aware of where the scenes are going, but our attention is focused on the details we see in our head as the scenes unfold and the characters' attitudes develop. In this way, our scenes fit together but are also dynamically alive. As Aristotle puts it in his *Poetics*, a writer should first outline and then keep the emerging scenes before his "eyes as much as possible. That way, seeing most vividly, as if he were actually getting close to the events as they happen, the poet can devise the appropriate 'business,' and discrepancies are least likely to escape his notice."[4]

This generous mode of attentiveness is called *soft focus* and is the opposite of hard focus, which is attending to just one thing. When we create generously, we soft focus our attention rather than hard focus it. Our attention is inclusive, not exclusive. We act like generous walkers in an airport, focused on finding our gate but peripherally aware of what is happening around us as we move around other people—not banging into their luggage, not tripping on the walkways, and so on.

With a soft focus, we can create an outline for a story and then push it to the back of our mind as we focus on creating the details of the story. In no way does the outline determine the details. For when we create generously, with a soft focus on our prior plans, we can't determine beforehand what our creation will turn out to be. In the process of creating the details, we may even need to revise the outline. For we can't hold our intentions (or what we are trying to do) fixed as we act—we have to revise our intentions *as* we act.

The fact that the details aren't determined by our outline doesn't mean some other force is determining them. It means nothing is determining them, not even our own past objectives. We create freely, drawing on our past objectives and the objectives of those around us, making explicit what is implicit in some of them, leaving implicit what we and others can make explicit in future efforts. We are creative only because the potentialities of the world continually outstrip its actualities. There is always more to say about the world than can be said.

## Your Pitch

The first outline you need to create for your story is a one-sentence statement called a pitch. A pitch is what you might say to friends when you tell them you saw a good movie and they ask you what it is about. The word comes from the phrase "sales pitch." But for writers, a pitch isn't simply a marketing device; it is a way of organizing a story. A pitch states the main character's main line of action—the main thing the main character is trying to do—and how the main character develops in the process—the types of choices he makes in trying to carry out the action. Here is a pitch for a possible movie of *The Three Little Pigs,* courtesy of Mel Henderson, a creative teaching assistant of mine (who is doing the assignments at the end of the chapters with Madeleine): *The Three Little Pigs* is a comedy, set in a small New Jersey town, about Lou, a clever but greedy pig wanting to have his cake and eat it too, who tries to exploit his kind-hearted but dim-witted younger brothers and learns that greed will deprive him of his "cake" and of his brothers too.

Notice the elements of the pitch:

- The name of the movie (*The Three Little Pigs*)
- The genre (comedy)
- The setting (a small New Jersey town)
- The main character (a pig named Lou)
- The initial characterization (a clever but greedy pig wanting to have his cake and eat it too)
- The main character's main line of action (exploit his kind-hearted but dim-witted brothers)
- The final characterization (realizes his greed has deprived him of the cake and his brothers)

You can write a pitch for your movie in three stages. First, write the main character's main line of action, which is a statement of the main action your main character is trying to carry out. (It is not a list of the things he does. It is a statement of the main action he is pursuing.) He may be pursuing more than one line of action—like getting the gold and getting the girl—but one of them needs to be the main one. The main one is the plot; the others are subplots. For the *Three Little Pigs,* the main line of action is this: A pig tries to exploit his kind-hearted but dim-witted younger brothers.

Second, include the initial and final characterizations—the character traits that indicate, as Aristotle would put it, the types of choices your character makes in beginning the action and in finishing or abandoning it.[5] (A characterization is not just a list of character traits. Though the pig may be witty, prone to giggle, clever, and basically happy as the story starts, and bitter, antagonistic, and realizing his loss when the story ends, only "clever but greedy" and "realizing his loss" provide an initial and final characterization for the character development in this line of action, because only they describe the types of choices he makes in his main action.) Here is the pitch now: A clever but greedy pig wanting to have his cake and eat it too, tries to exploit his kind-hearted but dim-witted younger brothers and learns that greed will deprive him of his "cake" and of his brothers too.

Third, include the name of the movie, the genre, the name of the main character, and the setting: *The Three Little Pigs* is a comedy, set in a small New Jersey town, about Lou, a clever but greedy pig wanting to have his cake and eat it too, who tries to exploit his kind-hearted but dim-witted younger brothers and learns that greed will deprive him of his "cake" and of his brothers too.

The resulting pitch has the following form: [The name of the movie] is a [genre of the movie], set in [the setting], about [the name of the main character], a [the initial characterization], who is trying to [the action] and comes to learn [the final characterization].

The pitch about Lou could be abbreviated, say for a TV guide, into what is called a logline, something like this: A clever pig tries to outwit his dim-witted brothers. It is not as interesting as the full pitch but is still intriguing. The most engaging loglines allow us to infer some of the main elements of the pitches. Here are four actual loglines from movies:

(1)   A reckless cop struggles to save his estranged wife when terrorists overtake her office building (*Die Hard*).

Notice that this logline has an initial characterization (reckless and estranged from his wife) and what the character is trying to do (save his wife). We can infer the likely character development (he becomes less reckless and estranged), the setting (contemporary), and the genre (action/drama.)

(2)   When her sister is kidnapped, a timid romance novelist ventures to South America to save her (*Romancing the Stone*).

In this one, we are given the initial characterization (timid but interested in romance) and can infer an ending characterization (this character will become less timid and find romance). We can infer that this is an action film because

**Minority Report, 2002**

kidnappers are involved. Notice the contrast between the initial characterization (timid) and the line of action (save her sister from kidnappers): this type of contrast makes a pitch more interesting and occurs in the best of them.

(3)  In a future where criminals are arrested before the crime occurs, a despondent cop struggles on the lam to prove his innocence for a murder he has not yet committed (*Minority Report*).

This one has most of the elements of a full pitch: setting (future), initial characterization (despondent and on the lam), and line of action of the main character (trying to prove his innocence). If we can infer that the film is a drama and that this character becomes less despondent and more able to work within the system, we have it all.

(4)  After a series of grisly shark attacks, a sheriff struggles to protect his small beach community against the bloody monster, in spite of the greedy chamber of commerce (*Jaws*).

This logline states the action, but it doesn't include anything about character development. I leave it to you to decide if this omission is a defect of the pitch or the film itself.

A good pitch can convince people that they will enjoy reading and watching the story. It tells them that the story is (1) unique enough that they could understand something new and significant (how would a timid person rescue her sister?), and (2) familiar enough that their previous experiences could help them understand and care about the main character and what that character

**Jaws, 1975**

is trying to do (haven't we all had to prove we were innocent of something?). If you can't write this kind of pitch for your script, you need to pick a different story to write. Without a good pitch, you won't get anyone to publish your novel or fund and distribute your film. The pitch is that important. If *you* can't express your story in one simple, engaging line, readers and viewers certainly won't be able to, which means they won't be able to tell their friends and family about your story in a way that gets them interested in it. A novel or film that can't be sold by word of mouth has little to offer a publisher or producer.

## Audience Test

Once you have written some possible pitches, you should audience test them. Simply present them to people and ask them to respond to the following statements on a scale from one to five—one meaning they strongly disagree, and five meaning they strongly agree. You may want to include other statements as well. Keep track of the gender and age ranges of your respondents: 5–15, 16–25, 26–55, 56+.

- I think I will experience something new and significant in this novel and film

- I think I will care about what the main character is trying to do
- I think I would like to read this novel and see the movie when it comes out

As you compile their scored responses, a strong leader will likely emerge.

## The Next Chapter

In this chapter, you have summarized your story in a one-sentence pitch about your main character's main line of action and character development in that line of action. In the next chapter, you will flesh out your pitch with summaries of the scenes in that main line of action. The result will be a synopsis of your story.

## Student Writing Group

### Week Four

1. Read the introduction and assignments, and write your questions. Then read the chapter, and write your answers.

   *You say that a pitch is a one-sentence summary. But I always thought a pitch meant a really awesome tagline. So how much of a summary does the pitch have to be?* The pitch should include the name of the movie, the genre, the setting, the main character's main line of action, and the initial and final characterization of the main character in that line of action. If my pitch includes these elements, it will spark interest and give enough away to allow advertisement by word of mouth. Mel suggests that I imagine I'm dealing with an impatient producer. He tells me, "You have twenty seconds of my attention. Give me the basics, the heart of the story—and we'll see if I want to extend your twenty seconds."

2. Find pitches online for two movies you like, and write them down. Bear in mind that the ones you find online aren't likely to be as informative as those you will learn to write in this chapter.

   Pitch for *The Hours:* The story of how the novel "Mrs. Dalloway" affects three generations of women, all of whom, in one way or another, have had to deal with suicide in their lives.

   Pitch for *Speed Racer:* With support from Pops and Mom Racer, girlfriend Trixie, younger brother Spritle, and the mysterious Racer X, Speed takes on fierce competitors to save his family's business and protect the sport he loves.

3. Write at least two pitches for the story you are writing.

   Mel and I created four pitches for *Against a Crooked Sky*:

(1) *Against a Crooked Sky* is a postapocalyptic, action-adventure film about a fourteen-year-old boy's determined quest to rescue his captured sister from a modern tribe of Aztec restorationists led by a former doctor of Meso-American theology and archaeology.

(2) *Against a Crooked Sky* is a postapocalyptic action-adventure film about a cocky, headstrong fourteen-year-old boy trying to rescue his kidnapped sister from a tribe of modern Aztec restorationists, who learns, with the help of a cynical former CIA agent, that sacrifice doesn't go unnoticed.

(3) *Against a Crooked Sky* is a postapocalyptic, action-adventure film set in the western United States about a fourteen-year-old boy who unflinchingly pursues his sister's abductors in order to rescue her from an uncertain fate among a modern tribe of Aztec restorationists and who survives this savage new world with the help of a crusty former CIA agent.

(4) *Against a Crooked Sky* is a postapocalyptic, romantic, musical, western horror-mystery-suspense-thriller docudrama. A definite must–see!!!!

4. Audience test your pitches to find out which of them is strongest. Email at least six people, write a paragraph summarizing your experience with your respondents, and explain how this feedback can help you.

Mel and I hassled a bunch of people in our email address book until they agreed to read our pitches. We asked them to respond to the following statements on a scale of one to five, one meaning they strongly disagree and five meaning they strongly agree:

I think I will experience something new and significant in this novel and film

I think I will care about what the main character is trying to do
I think I would like to read this novel and see the movie when it comes out
Here were the average scores:

Pitch 1: 1.5
Pitch 2: 4 (the definite favorite)
Pitch 3: 2.5
Pitch 4: 0

From this exercise, we realized that Pitch 1 offers too much unimportant detail, and Pitch 2 gives more interesting story information—it is the only pitch that includes both the action and the initial and final characterizations. By the way, our favorite response was this one: "No offense, but number 4 seems like it's trying too hard to cover every possible genre." No kidding—you picked up on that!

# Synopsis

Now that you have written a one-sentence pitch, it is time to expand your pitch into a five- or six-page summary called a synopsis. In this chapter, you will write a detailed synopsis for your script and film novel. Your synopsis will summarize just the scenes that show the action of your pitch – the main character's main line of action. Then you will audience test your synopsis.

### Week Five

1. Read the introduction and assignments, and write your questions. Then read the chapter, and write your answers.
2. State the main line of action of a movie you like. Then summarize four key scenes in that line of action: the beginning scene, two scenes with major turning points, and the final scene.
3. Write a synopsis for your story by doing the following: (a) Write down your pitch. (b) Write a one-paragraph summary of each scene in your main character's main line of action. The main line of action should have at least twenty scenes, including at least two scenes with major turning points that create act breaks. Indicate the act breaks with horizontal lines. (c) Write a statement of the theme – a sentence indicating what the character development in the main line of action is about.
4. Audience test your synopsis, emailing at least six people. Summarize your experiences with your respondents, and explain how this feedback can help you.

## Glossary

**turning point**   A main change in the action of a character
**key scenes**   The beginning scene, at least two middle scenes with major turning points, and the ending scene in a line of action
**acts**   The main units of a story, separated by major turning points
**theme**   What the insights or decisive choices of characters are fundamentally about

A pitch states the main character's main line of action. The synopsis starts with the pitch, summarizes the scenes that show the action of the pitch, and finishes with a theme that summarizes the character development that takes place in the main line of action. The synopsis provides the spine for a script and novel. It contains summaries of at least twenty scenes, including (1) a beginning scene that starts the main character's main line of action, (2) middle scenes with major turning points that create act breaks, and (3) an ending scene in which the action is completed or abandoned.

**Charles Peirce**

## Line of Action

A line of action is an overall action a main character carries out by means of a series of small actions. For example, John's line of action may be to marry Martha, but he does this by moving out of his parents' house, finding he doesn't like being alone, noticing Martha in the apartment lobby, overcoming his shyness ... and at the altar saying, "I do." Each small action suggests the overall action and makes possible the next small action. The opening scene doesn't need to make the overall action obvious to readers – just suggest it.

**Bicycle Thieves, 1948**

There are two main ways of making the scenes in a line of action engaging. The first is to only suggest what the line of action is at the beginning. Then we engage our readers in trying to figure out what the character is up to, what he is fundamentally trying to do. If we don't let our readers know what the overall action is at the beginning, then we probably shouldn't let the character himself know either. Otherwise, our readers won't be able to sympathize with the character. At the end of the line of action, we let the character "constitute [his] behavior as a completed action," as one theorist puts it.[1] That means we give our readers enough information about the character that they could state what the overall line of action was. Such a statement of the overall action becomes what philosopher Charles Peirce calls "an abridged statement of the way [the character] has … evolved."[2] Let's look at an example.

*Bicycle Thieves* is a movie about a man who searches for his stolen bicycle, which he needs for his work. He takes his son with him, reassuring the boy that they will find it. When he can't find the bicycle, he sends the boy home, steals another man's bicycle, and is caught by people nearby. The boy hears the commotion and returns. The man is so ashamed in front of the boy that the people decide to let him go. In the final scene, the man walks away with the boy, who in deep sadness takes his father's hand.

What is the father's main line of action in this film? Theorists like Robert McKee would see the father as having two main lines of action – one he is conscious of and one he is not conscious of.[3] The one he is conscious of is trying to find his bicycle; the deeper one he is not conscious of is trying to preserve his dignity as a man in front of his son. Since the father isn't conscious of this deeper action he is engaged in, he must, McKee would claim, be subconsciously aware of it.

**Andre Bazin**

But there is another way of looking at the action of the father. Film critic Andre Bazin, drawing on Sartre's dictum that existence precedes essence, writes about the father's action in *Bicycle Thieves,* "The action does not exist beforehand as if it were an essence." In other words, the nature of the father's action as he looks for his bicycle isn't established – either consciously or subconsciously in the mind of the main character – at the beginning of the film. Instead, the nature or "essence" of what the father is doing emerges along the way. Using language similar to Peirce's, Bazin writes, "The action is assembled – less in terms of 'tension' than of a 'summation' of the events."[4] In the beginning, viewers (and the father) think he is just trying to find his bicycle. Later, they realize that more fundamentally he has been trying to preserve his dignity as a man, first by trying to find his bicycle and second by stealing one. So the father's line of action isn't what he has consciously or subconsciously been pursuing from the beginning – it is what at the end we see he has done.

The scenes in *Bicycle Thieves* don't engage viewers by simply increasing their suspense about whether or not the father will find the bicycle. Instead, they invite viewers to try to understand what the nature of the father's main action is. And it is more engaging for viewers to have to interpret along the way what a character is really doing than to just wonder whether or not he will complete his action.

A second way of making the scenes in a line of action engaging is to create turning points. A turning point changes the potentialities of the next actions. It is an action or event that makes carrying out the overall action harder or easier, more significant, or different in nature. A turning point might occur, for example, when John calls Martha, hoping to take her to a movie, and Martha tells him she is quite tired. That is an opportunity for John to generously synthesize new possibilities – a turning point.

Turning points create emotions in our characters and our readers who empathize with them. At turning points, the situations our characters face change, and these changes disrupt them from smoothly carrying out the actions they have been pursuing. As a result, our characters, trying to synthesize new possibilities for action, may feel grief, joy, or fear, for example, and our readers will likely empathize with them. Turning points also create suspense for readers, raising questions about what our characters will do next, given the new potentialities created by the situations, people, and problems they face. The suspense shouldn't simply be about who will win as two forces duke it out in a chase scene or a fight; it should be about the choices our characters will make. These questions may arise and soon be answered, or the suspense may continue for some time. Those situations need to keep changing.

A line of action with turning points is a story with a beginning, a middle, and an end, to use Aristotle's terminology. What is a beginning? Most contemporary instructors (like Syd Field and Robert McKee) think it means a stretch before the action starts, a setup – what McKee thinks of as an initial equilibrium[5] – which ends when an inciting incident disrupts the equilibrium and starts the action (the setup and inciting incident often being called the first act). The ending is then what happens after the action is over, the denouement – the reestablishment of equilibrium. But this interpretation is a misunderstanding of Aristotle's *Poetics,* and it results in stories that start slow and end slow.

A beginning, Aristotle explains, is "that which does not necessarily follow on something else, but after it something else naturally is or happens." So a beginning isn't what comes before the action starts. It is a way of starting the action. An end "is that which naturally follows on something else, either necessarily or for the most part, but nothing else after it." So the end isn't what comes after the action is over but a way of ending the action. And a middle is "that which naturally follows on something else and something else on it."[6]

In other words, a beginning is a scene that starts the action in a way that the audience can understand and appreciate without having to understand something that happened before it. So the beginning scene of a story couldn't be, for example, someone coming out screaming and crying – we couldn't feel for the person without knowing more background – but it could be someone looking distraught at a stack of bills. The middle scenes are those the audience can't fully understand and appreciate without understanding what comes before and after them. They could include, for example, the distraught person looking at an old family photo and starting to weep. An ending scene is one the audience can understand and appreciate without having to understand something that happens later. The ending scene, for example, could be this weeping person encountering a friend and talking about the relative in the photo and becoming more composed.

For Aristotle, the denouement is the untying of the problem after it has been tied up. It is what happens after the plot has most fully thickened until the end when it is resolved.[7] It isn't what comes after the action is over. When the action is over, the play or movie is over.

## Theme

A line of action is meaningful when it ends up completed or abandoned and concludes with a significant insight or character-changing choice; we don't want to count a sequence of events as a line of action unless it concludes with an insight or decisive choice. "The characters' actions build up to that moment of change," creative writing teacher Sybil Johnston writes[8]. The decisive choice or realization is "the story's climax," what the sequence of scenes "leads to," what the story is about, "why [the] story matters."[9] This change in a character needn't be "obvious or easily summarized, [but] if the story is well told, it can be felt."[10]

The word insight indicates a change in belief, but not just any change. An insight is a belief in something true and significant. Insight, like knowledge, presupposes success: the insights and knowledge we have must be true. We could say a character believes the world is flat, but we couldn't say he knows it is flat, since it isn't flat. In other words, if we say a character comes to an insight, we must also believe his insight.

A decisive choice is like knowledge or insight. It is choosing something that, in some sense, is right and true. Philosopher Martin Heidegger tried to find a term for such choices. He used the term "*disclosive*" – because these choices open up new horizons of thinking and behaving.[11] The choices that open up these productive possibilities may be as diverse as "the act that founds a political state," an act of "sacrifice," or a "thinker's questioning."[12] Any such action that opens up productive possibilities constitutes the character change we are looking for at the end of a line of action. A character needn't develop from a bad person to a good person or a good person to a better person. A character just needs to do something that creates a new horizon of possibilities.

When a character comes to a decisive choice or insight at the end of a line of action, it is natural to end the story – but not because the character has found a truth that wraps everything up and halts action. Instead, insights and decisive choices open up new worlds of action. The story comes to an end because a new story for the character has become possible.

If we write generously about the insights and decisive choices our characters come to, we re-understand our own world and learn something. Then when our readers take our characters' new attitudes seriously and synthesize them with their own, empathetically finding some aspect of them right and worth preserving, they too learn. Poet Janet St. John states, "What often makes a piece of writing shine? That the writer learns something personally, or about the world, and the reader inevitably also learns through the process of reading that work."[13] We and our readers may even learn more than our characters do. What we learn from their insights and decisive choices is the theme of our story.

We have an idea of the theme once we write our pitch – the final characterization is the germ of the theme. As we write, we keep this theme, like the plot, in the back of our minds and focus our attention on our characters and what they are doing and thinking and coming to understand in their scenes. The theme guides our writing without dominating it. As we develop the story, we come to a better understanding of the final characterization and the theme based on it. In this way, our theme develops as we write the story.

While our theme emerges from the development of our characters, we can also shape the various stylistic elements of our story to help bring the theme out. These elements include patterns of repetition and variation, montages, narration, interior monologue, flashbacks, flash-forwards, and imagined scenes. As a result, the burden of conveying the theme won't rest solely on the actions and dialogue of the characters: we won't have to put unnatural words in the mouths of our characters or have them perform unbelievable actions to convey the theme. (Nor will the burden rest solely on the elements of style themselves: we won't need, for example, a long-winded, reflective narrator.) Together, the stylistic elements and the characters' action and dialogue will share the burden of helping the viewer understand what the character development is fundamentally about.

Once we have written a draft of a story, it is important to ask readers for their interpretation of the theme, not to make sure our own interpretations are coming across, but to compare their interpretations with ours. Generous writers hope to find diverse but consistent interpretations. The theme should be neither obvious (inviting the same interpretations) nor obscure (inviting inconsistent interpretations). "I am usually happiest," Sibyl Johnston explains, "when the reader sees something slightly different from but consistent with what I see. I think this indicates that the scene is alive at a level deeper than my consciousness. On the other hand, if the two versions are contradictory, [I] may need to clarify."[14]

**Yoshi Oida**

Acting teacher Yoshi Oida agrees that stories should elicit different but consistent interpretations. He is at pains, he explains, to teach his acting students to avoid the "conventional image," "the clichéd image."[15] But he also writes, "In the Noh theatre, they have a saying: 'You must unify one thousand eyes.' This means that the fundamental points of your performance should have the same impact on all the onlookers. Everyone should basically agree about what they are seeing."[16] When a story invites diverse but basically consistent interpretations, the story gains an objectivity, an existence independent of any of its readers. When it doesn't invite diverse but consistent interpretations – when readers find the theme or meaning of the story obvious or obscure – the story needs to be rewritten.

## Your Synopsis

You can now write a synopsis for your story. Start with your pitch, and conclude with a statement of your theme. In between, write a paragraph summarizing each scene in your main line of action. Make sure each scene, except the last, leaves readers wondering what the main character will do next. And make sure what the main character does in each scene, except the first, grows out of what the characters have done in earlier scenes. You should have at least twenty scenes in your main line of action, including the following four key scenes:

1. A beginning scene, which conveys an idea of the main character's main line of action and the initial characterization of the main character in that line of action.
2. A scene with the first major turning point in the line of action, which ends the first act.
3. A scene with the second major turning point, which ends the second act.
4. An ending scene, which completes or abandons the line of action and reveals the ending characterization – the main character's insight or decisive choice.

If you have more than three acts (or two major turning points), you need more than four key scenes. You need a key scene for every major turning point.

You may want to write summaries of these four key scenes first and then add the other scenes. Remember, for now, you just want the scenes for your main character's main line of action. If you have other scenes you would like to include, save them somewhere. You may be able to use them when you add in other lines of action in the next chapter.

Here is a simple synopsis that develops the pitch for *The Three Little Pigs* that we read in the last chapter. The horizontal lines come after the major turning points in the synopsis and indicate act breaks. Notice how every scene is told from Lou's perspective and moves him closer or further away from completing his line of action.

[Pitch] *The Three Little Pigs* is a comedy about Lou, a clever but greedy pig in a small New Jersey town who tries to have his cake and eat it too by exploiting his kind-hearted but dim-witted younger brothers and learns that greed will deprive him of his "cake" and of his brothers too.

[Beginning scene, with opening characterization of Lou] The story begins as Lou turns off the Xbox gaming console and talks to his brothers about making a change in their lives. Lou persuades them to pursue their dreams and assures his brothers he'll help them. Frankie wants to open his own recreation and rehabilitation center for recovering addicts; Rocco wants to open his own pizza restaurant.

The brothers pool all their money and divide it three ways. Lou agrees to handle the money for them, and they're off.

Lou builds his home of the finest and most fashionable materials with all the bells and whistles, wanting a home that will appraise high and be a good investment.

[First major turning point, ending Act 1] Lou spends so much money on his glamorous home that he has little left for the roof and uses cheap shingles. This doesn't bother him; he figures no one really ever sees the roof. He dreams of the "windfall" that will come to him.

---

Later, the two brothers enter Lou's home in full panic. Lou tells them to calm down as they try to explain the situation to their big brother.

Lou notices a wolf outside, and the wolf threatens to blow down his house. Lou laughs and invites the wolf to try.

After repeated unsuccessful attempts, the wolf finds a trellis and climbs to the roof.

Suspecting the wolf is headed for the chimney, Lou immediately starts a fire in the fireplace, and the brothers gather around it, waiting for signs of the wolf's descent.

[Second major turning point, ending Act 2] On the roof, the wolf sits on the stone chimney and strikes a match, then drops it. The shingles burst into flames, and the wolf cackles with delight, safe on his stony perch.

---

The brothers sit anxiously huddled at the fireplace, waiting for the wolf's next move and trying to guess what he'll do. Lou suddenly realizes that something has gone awry. He lamely excuses himself, saying he has to check on a cake in the oven.

But he is actually retrieving insurance documents on all the brothers' property and cash from a hidden safe. He tucks these into his jacket where they can't be seen and returns to stand by his brothers.

Moments later, the flimsy roof implodes – crashing down in a burst of ash. Luckily, no one is harmed, but the pigs hear low laughter above their heads and look up. The wolf calls down to Lou, asking if he has his fifty percent. Lou hollers that he has never seen the wolf in his life. Just then, the doorbell rings.

Lou's neighbor, who sold Lou the homeowner's insurance, explains to Rocco and Frankie that someone has victimized them in an insurance fraud scheme, and that someone is their brother Lou. In that instant, all the men realize that Lou has fled.

[Ending scene, with ending characterization of Lou] Some time later, Lou and the wolf stand, heads down, in a white-collar penitentiary cafeteria line. A passing prisoner taunts Lou about his insurance fraud scheme. Lou ignores him, but the hotheaded wolf takes the bait and taunts back. As Lou advances in line, an off-camera worker asks, "Hey buddy – you want cake too?" Lou looks up and then back down.

The theme is this: greed has a high price.

## Audience Test

Once you have written your synopsis, you can audience test it. Email it to your friends, leaving off the theme at the end, and ask them to respond to the following statements, again on a scale of one to five, one meaning they strongly disagree and five meaning they strongly agree.

### As the story began:

1. I began to care about the main character
2. I had some idea of what the main character was trying to do
3. I had some idea of how the main character might develop

### As the story developed:

4. I cared more about the main character
5. I better understood the nature, difficulty, and importance of what the main character was trying to do
6. I had a better idea of how the main character was developing
7. Each scene left me wondering what the main character would do next
8. What the main character did in each scene grew out of what the characters did in earlier scenes
9. I noticed several major turning points in what the main character was trying to do

### As the story ended:

10. I didn't feel manipulated
11. I cared about the main character significantly more that I did in the beginning
12. I understood how the main character completed or abandoned his pursuit

13. I believe the main character finally came to an insight or decisive choice
14. I value the insight or decisive choice the main character came to
15. I can state a theme based on the insight or decisive choice the main character came to:

---------------------------------------------------

You should rework your synopsis and audience test it again (1) if you get strong disagreements on these statements or (2) if you don't get diverse but consistent statements of the theme. Don't expect your readers to tell you how to fix problems in your synopsis – most people don't know how to fix story problems. But they can tell you if there are problems. Then it is up to you and your writing team to figure out how to fix them.

## The Next Chapter

In this chapter, you summarized the scenes in your main character's main line of action. In the next chapter, you will summarize the scenes in your supporting lines of action. The result will be a scenario – a summary of all the scenes for your script and novel.

## Student Writing Group

### Week Five

1. Read the introduction and assignments, and write your questions. Then read the chapter, and write your answers.

   *What is a line of action? Is it a string of scenes that feature the main character?* Not exactly. A line of action is one main action that is brought about by a string of smaller actions carried out by the main character. But you don't know the line of action unless you know the entire story. Moses' line of action was to free his people from Egypt and from sin, but he definitely didn't know that at the beginning of *The Ten Commandments*. For Pete's sake, he was just a baby.

2. State the main line of action of a movie you like. Then summarize four key scenes in that line of action: the beginning scene, two scenes with major turning points, and the final scene.

   Main Line of Action for *Speed Racer*: Speed Racer topples Royalton Industries to protect his family and purify the sport of car racing.

   Opening Scene: Speed Racer wins another race but purposefully maintains his older brother's record on that race, demonstrating that the memory of his brother (who secretly fought against Royalton as well) still haunts him.

Major Turning Point: Royalton reveals to Speed Racer that car racing is not a pure sport; the outcomes of the races are predetermined by greedy corporations.

Major Turning Point: Taejo Togokahn doesn't hand over his files that connect Royalton to criminals, reneging on his promise.

Closing Scene: Speed Racer wins the Grand Prix and accepts the (for once) rightfully won trophy.

3. Write a synopsis for your story by doing the following: (a) Write down your pitch. (b) Write a one-paragraph summary of each scene in your main character's main line of action. The main line of action should have at least twenty scenes, including at least two scenes with major turning points that create act breaks. Indicate the act breaks with horizontal lines. (c) Write a statement of the theme – a sentence indicating what the character development in the main line of action is about.

Here we go! But due to publishing constraints, I'm only going to include Act One of the synopsis.

*Against a Crooked Sky* is a postapocalyptic, action-adventure film about a cocky, headstrong fourteen-year-old boy who tries to rescue his kidnapped sister from a tribe of modern Aztec restorationists – whose secret sanctuary he can find only with the help of a cynical former CIA agent with secrets of his own – and learns that sacrifice isn't just giving something up to help someone – it is opening the way for others to do what you can't.

It is spring 2022 in a highly organized, fenced-in community named Liberty in the western states region, where Sam Sutter plays cards with three of his buddies (Nathan, Jake, and Mike) in a fort lookout, shirking his duties. Sam wins hand after hand in the game and declares to his friends that he was born to win. Nathan says he should get back to work. Sam tells him to stop worrying – he'll get his job done in time. When Sam's sister, Charlotte, comes looking for him, the boys duck out of sight. Mike remarks how "hot" Charlotte is, angering Sam, but the situation is silently diffused by Nathan. After Charlotte leaves, Sam glances beyond the safe confines of the community gates to see a lone figure approaching, haggard and in distress. The figure falls. Sam abandons his game and runs to get his sister.

Lyman Sutter, Sam's father, is spearheading preparations for a rescue effort to retrieve the group of refugees the injured man comes from. Learning that his sister plans to join the team, Sam tries to persuade his father to let him go in her stead. He wants to be treated like an adult, and he is truly concerned about her safety out there. Lyman refuses; they need Charlotte's medical skills. Sam angrily suggests that Lyman will likely be too busy "saving the world" to protect his own daughter. Lyman hotly dismisses Sam. The Hawkins brothers teasingly assure Sam that they'll "keep a good eye on" Charlotte. Sam determines to do whatever it takes to go along. He submissively returns to Lyman and promises to perform any task in absolute obedience if he can go too. Lyman and Ellie, Sam's mother, agree it may be good for Sam to go – Sam is "too big for his britches." Ellie gives Sam an emergency whistle and demonstrates a signal – three sharp blows – "so your dad knows it's you." Sam is embarrassed. She insists that he wear it at all times.

When they reach the injured refugees, Sam does as he's told and collects firewood. He is uncomfortable in the face of so much suffering and sobers up a little.

Charlotte joins Sam by a fire, and he feels better with her nearby. She asks him what he thinks of the world "outside of Liberty." Sam tells her that staying safe is just a matter of controlling fear and being "smart." Charlotte assures him that a person is always safe and protected when he is doing God's will. Unconvinced, Sam asks her, "What if it isn't God's will to keep him safe?" Before she can answer, Lyman calls them to bed.

The next morning, Charlotte asks Sam to go to the falls with her to wash up. No one in camp is to go anywhere alone. He suggests she hurry and catch up with her friends – he just heard them leave. Charlotte agrees but says if they aren't at the falls she's coming back to get him. Sam promises to go with her in that case and turns his attention to his breakfast. When his whistle clanks against his plate, he takes it off and lays it aside.

Not seeing her friends at the falls, Charlotte begins to turn back. She hears a hidden woman calling for help. She tries to find her but discovers she's been tricked: she is suddenly abducted by three strangers on horseback. She reaches for her whistle, but one of her attackers tears it from her neck and throws it down. At breakfast, Sam absentmindedly returns the greeting of Charlotte's two friends, who he thought were at the falls. He suddenly realizes that Charlotte must be alone. He abandons his plate and bolts, arriving at the falls just in time to see Charlotte being taken. He calls and runs after her, fumbling for his whistle, and then realizes in horror that he took it off. But he still runs. Spotting Charlotte's whistle in the mud, he grabs it and gives three sharp blows in the direction of camp. He runs after the abductors, repeating his whistle signal, hoping to not lose their trail before help arrives on horseback.

The theme (which makes more sense at the end of the complete synopsis) is this: A sacrifice has a powerful effect.

4. Audience test your synopsis, emailing at least six people. Summarize your experiences with your respondents, and explain how this feedback can help you.

> The statement I consistently got low scores on was, "I began to care about the main character," and I got consistently high scores on the statement, "I had some idea of what the main character was trying to do." Perhaps this is because the main character (Sam) is too clichéd, making him annoying or, even worse, boring. But being easy to nail down also makes him predictable, which would be why it was easy for my reviewers to understand what Sam was trying to do from the start. So it looks as though I need to rethink the complexity of my main character. The other statements got positive reviews, so plotwise, we seem to be doing okay. Gimme five, Mel!

# Scenario

Now it is time to expand your summary from a five- or six-page synopsis to a fifteen- to twenty-page scenario. In this chapter, which will take you two weeks to work through, you will add other lines of action to your main one – opposing lines of action and supporting ones. The opposing lines of action will complicate and make more difficult the main character's main line of action. The supporting lines of action will move forward or make more significant the main character's main line of action. Then you will write scene summaries for these lines of action and weave them into a scenario. You will then evaluate your scenario in three ways: (1) You will put your scene summaries into a scenario chart to make sure each line of action is strong. (2) You will write a two-page trailer to see if your scenario has enough interesting moments to make your story marketable. (3) Finally, you will audience test your scenario. With these three evaluations, you will have an idea of how to revise your scenario.

### Week Six

1. Read the introduction to this chapter and the assignments for weeks six and seven. Write your questions; then read the chapter, and write your answers.
2. Write down the lines of action in the movie you wrote key scenes for in the last chapter. For each line of action, write one sentence that includes the action, the initial characterization, and the final characterization.

3. Write down the main line of action and the opposing and supporting lines of action for the film novel you are writing. For each line of action, write one sentence that includes the action, the initial characterization, and the final characterization.
4. Write down the theme of your film novel. Make sure it fits with the final characterizations in your lines of action, each final characterization bringing out something that complements or contrasts with the theme. Rewrite the theme if necessary.

### Week Seven

1. Write a scenario for your script and novel by doing the following: (a) Write a one-paragraph summary of each scene in your opposing and supporting lines of action, and weave these summaries into the scene summaries for your main line of action. Indicate in brackets, at the beginning of each scene summary, which lines of action the scene is a part of. Make sure each scene moves the lines of action it is a part of either forward or backward. For each line of action, include summaries of one or two scenes with major turning points. Some of these major turning points should occur near the main act breaks you established for your main line of action. Use bold horizontal lines to indicate act breaks.(b) Write a one-sentence statement of the theme at the end.
2. Abbreviate your scene summaries and put them in a scenario chart. Make sure each line of action is well developed. Revise if necessary.
3. Write a two-minute trailer for your film. If you don't have the makings of an engaging trailer, revise your scenario.
4. Audience test your scenario, emailing at least six people. Summarize your experiences with your respondents, and explain how this feedback can help you.

### Glossary

**gaps**      Jumps in time that require readers to interpret what has happened in the interim
**scenario**  The sequence of summarized scenes in a script or novel

The final summary we need to write is called a *scenario*. A scenario is a sequence of summarized scenes for a script or novel. Typically, a producer is willing to pay as much for a scenario as for a completed script. The scenario – with its carefully worked out sequencing of scenes – is *that* important. The scenario serves both as an outline for the script, keeping us organized as we write, and as a mini-draft, inspiring us as we write scenes. If we take care with a scenario, it will rest solidly in the back of our minds, and we will be able to move the overall action forward while focusing our attention on writing the details of what our characters are doing and saying in their scenes.

## Multiple Lines of Action

Tootsie, 1982

Unlike short stories, which typically have just one line of action, engaging scripts and novels usually have multiple lines of action. Henry Green, a British novelist who wrote long, film-like novels, believed that to avoid being "flat," all script-like stories and novels should have multiple lines of action.[1] Films usually do. The film *Tootsie,* for example, has five lines of action, as script doctor Linda Seger explains. All but one are about the main character's relationship with someone or something: Michael finding work as an actor; Michael helping his insecure friend Sandy; Michael putting off the lecherous soap-opera doctor, Brewster; the soap-opera nurse, Julie, fending off the director, Ron; and Michael putting off Julie's father, who falls in love with him as a woman.[2] Each of these lines of action is like a separate story but functions like a thread in an overall tapestry.

Each line of action is important, but the main character's main line of action is crucial. It is the action in our pitch. It is the line of action that our other lines of action all need to relate to and support. If the main line of action is about a man getting the gold, then another line of action about him also getting the girl needs to continually impede or advance the one about him getting the gold. Lines of action about characters other than the main character should also connect to the main character's main line of action – that is, the other characters should oppose the main character or help him or bring out the significance of what the main character is trying to do.

Lines of action can be unified in the following ways:

- Many of the lines of action can be about the same character dealing with other characters or problems – like John dealing with Martha, with his job, with his father, etc.
- Every line of action can move forward or impede or bring out the significance of the main one.
- Each scene can link to the previous one, even if it comes from a different line of action. The Bible links scenes, Bar-Efrat explains, by "mentioning the same issue (person, event, action) at the end of one strand [scene] and at the beginning of the other."[3]
- Characters in one line of action can be connected to characters in another by messengers who inform them about what is happening in the other line of action. Bar-Efrat explains that the Bible does this – for example, messengers run from one army camp to another.
- Different lines of action can be kept in the minds of readers at the same time by characters in one line of action mentioning characters in other lines of action. Again, Bar-Efrat explains that the Bible does this.
- Each line of action can cover a few scenes before the next line of action is introduced, establishing itself in our minds before the new line of action starts up.
- The main character in a new line of action can be introduced in earlier scenes.
- Most of the lines of action can begin early in the story when the audience is sensing the scope of the story.
- Some scenes can be part of multiple lines of action, doing double duty.
- Major turning points in different lines of action can occur close to each other, reinforcing the act divisions for the main line of action.
- A theme can unify what the character development in the lines of action is fundamentally about, and scenes can be cut, revised, and added to in order to sustain the theme.

A good way to create a scenario is to completely fill out a main line of action first (which you did in the last chapter) and then fill out the other lines of

**As Good as it Gets, 1997**

action and weave them into the main one (which you will do in this chapter). The scenario will engage readers if it consists of a main line of action and a few supporting ones, each line of action having a changing, developing character.

Characters who don't change in attitude or situation don't engage readers in interpreting them. To be engaging, even hardened characters should show promise of changing by (1) acting with a little tenderness now and then, (2) having tenderhearted friends who hope for their change (as Laevsky has in *The Duel* or the Jack Nicholson character has in *As Good as it Gets*), or (3) suffering difficulties due to their own foolishness (like King Lear), which suggests change is coming.

Most films and novels have major turning points in each line of action, and these turning points come close together so that they create major parts or acts. A film or short novel will typically have two to five acts. If it has just one, the story may seem not to change enough. If there are more than five (which was Shakespeare's favorite number of acts), the story may seem to change too much. Most biblical narratives, Bar-Efrat explains, can be divided into two to ten acts – the story of Moses and the plagues in Egypt has ten.[4]

## Your Scenario

To write your scenario, first write down your one-sentence statements of what each line of action in your story is about. Start with your statement for your main character's main line of action. Make sure every other line of action sustains or impedes the main one. Include an action and an initial and final characterization for the character carrying out each line of action.

Here, for example, is a list of the lines of action for *The Three Little Pigs*, starting with the main one. Notice that each line of action has an initial and final characterization. The main characters are the pigs – Lou, Frankie, and Rocco – and the Wolf. But not all of them have lines of action, because some of them (like the Wolf) don't develop as characters.

Lou$_1$: Lou, a young, clever pig who values having his cake and eating it too, decides to get rich by exploiting his kind-hearted but dim-witted younger brothers and learns that greed will deprive him of his "cake" and his brothers too.

Lou$_2$: Lou works with a petty criminal to exploit his brother's trust and learns that thieves can't be relied on.

Frankie: Frankie, a young, simple pig trying to save money to open a recreation and rehab center, builds his home fast and cheap and learns that there are right ways to do good things.

Rocco: Rocco, a young, simple pig trying to save money to open a restaurant, builds his home carefully but with cheap materials and also learns that there are right ways to do good things.

Second, summarize the scenes in the new lines of action. Each line of action should have several scenes and should include the following: (1) the scene that begins the line of action and conveys the initial characterization, (2) at least one scene with a major turning point, and (3) the scene that

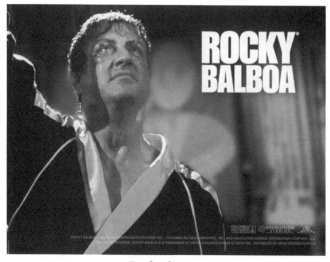

**Rocky, 1976**

ends the line of action (by completing or abandoning it) and conveys the final characterization with its significant insight or decisive choice. As you summarize each scene in these new lines of action, pick the character who changes most in the scene and try to describe the scene the way that character might. This will help you later turn the scenes into a script and a novel. Third, weave these new summaries into the summaries of the scenes in your main character's main line of action that you wrote in the last chapter. Begin and end your list of scenes with scenes from your main line of action, unless you think beginning or ending with scenes from an opposing or supporting line of action would better sustain the main line of action. (The movie *Rocky* begins with the romantic subplot, which provides a context for the main plot about boxing.) At the beginning of each scene, indicate which lines of action the scene is a part of. And at the end of the scenario, state the theme. Here are the summarized scenes for *The Three Little Pigs*. The horizontal lines indicate act breaks.

[Lou₁, Frankie, Rocco)] The story begins as Lou turns off the Xbox gaming console and talks to his brothers about making a change in their lives. Lou persuades them to pursue their dreams and assures his brothers he'll help them. Frankie wants to open his own recreation and rehabilitation center for recovering addicts; Rocco wants to open his own pizza restaurant.

[Lou₁, Frankie, Rocco] The brothers pool all their money and divide it three ways. Lou agrees to handle the money for them, and they're off.

[Frankie] Frankie builds his home of straw, reasoning that any money he saves building his house can be put toward his center. But he does pay for a solid roof.

[Rocco] Rocco builds his house of sticks, reasoning that any money he saves building his house can be put toward his pizza shop. But he does pay for a solid roof.

[Lou₁] Lou builds his home of the finest and most fashionable materials with all the bells and whistles, wanting a home that will appraise high and be a good investment.

[Lou₁] Lou spends so much money on his glamorous home that he has little left for the roof and uses cheap shingles. This doesn't bother him; he figures no one really ever sees the roof. He dreams of the "windfall" that will come to him.

---

[Frankie] Outside Frankie's straw house, the wolf demands to be let in. Frankie refuses, and the wolf says he will blow the house in – a sentiment Frankie misunderstands, as he encourages the wolf to say no to drugs.

[Frankie] As his home collapses, Frankie bolts out the back door toward Rocco's house.

[Frankie] Frankie's good, heavy roof falls to the ground, pinning the wolf's foot, delaying his pursuit.

[Frankie, Rocco] At Rocco's house, the wolf repeats his threat, which Rocco also misunderstands. He says his brother Frankie can give him some referrals for help.

[Frankie, Rocco] As his home collapses, Rocco races after Frankie out the back door toward Lou's house.

[Frankie, Rocco] Again, the heavy roof falls on the wolf's foot, delaying his pursuit.

[Frankie, Rocco, Lou$_1$] The two brothers enter Lou's home in full panic. Lou tells them to calm down as they try to explain the situation to their big brother.

[Frankie, Rocco, Lou$_1$, Lou$_2$] Lou notices a wolf outside, and the wolf repeats his threat for the third time. Lou laughs and invites the wolf to try to blow down his house.

[Frankie, Rocco, Lou$_1$, Lou$_2$] After repeated unsuccessful attempts, the wolf finds a trellis and climbs to the roof.

[Frankie, Rocco, Lou$_1$, Lou$_2$] Suspecting the wolf is headed for the chimney, Lou immediately starts a fire in the fireplace, and the brothers gather around it, waiting for signs of the wolf's descent.

[Frankie, Rocco, Lou$_1$, Lou$_2$] On the roof, the wolf sits on the stone chimney and strikes a match, then drops it. The shingles burst into flames, and the wolf cackles with delight, safe on his stony perch.

---

[Frankie, Rocco, Lou$_1$, Lou$_2$] The brothers sit anxiously huddled at the fireplace, waiting for the wolf's next move and trying to guess what he'll do. Lou suddenly realizes that something has gone awry. He lamely excuses himself, saying he has to check on a cake in the oven.

[Lou$_1$, Lou$_2$] But he is actually retrieving insurance documents on all the brothers' property and cash from a hidden safe. He tucks these into his jacket where they can't be seen and returns to stand by his brothers.

[Frankie, Rocco, Lou$_1$, Lou$_2$] Moments later, the flimsy roof implodes – crashing down in a burst of ash. Luckily, no one is harmed, but the pigs hear low laughter above their heads and look up. The wolf calls down to Lou, asking if he has his fifty percent. Lou hollers that he has never seen the wolf in his life. Just then, the doorbell rings.

[Frankie, Rocco, Lou$_1$, Lou$_2$] Lou's neighbor, who sold Lou the homeowner's insurance, explains to Rocco and Frankie that someone has

victimized them in an insurance fraud scheme, and that someone is
their brother Lou. In that instant, all the men realize that Lou has fled.
[Frankie, Rocco] The neighbor races to the door with Rocco and
Frankie close behind him.

[Frankie, Rocco, Lou$_2$] At the last moment, Frankie remembers the
troubled wolf perched silently on the chimney, and in his kind way,
naively offers him the only hospitality he can – telling the wolf that Lou
apparently left a cake in the oven so to help himself while they're gone.

[Frankie, Rocco, Lou$_2$] This tips off the neighbor, who knows the wolf
is a petty criminal, and the wolf is arrested.

[Lou$_1$, Lou$_2$] Some time later, Lou and the Wolf stand, heads down, in a
white-collar penitentiary cafeteria line. A passing prisoner taunts Lou about
his insurance fraud scheme. Lou ignores him, but the hot-headed wolf takes
the bait and taunts back. As Lou advances in line, an off-camera worker
asks, "Hey buddy – you want cake too?" Lou looks up and then back down.

[Frankie, Rocco] Back at Lou's house, which now has a strong new roof, we
see that Frankie and Rocco have helped each other reach their dreams: two
signs above the door read "Rocco's Vegan Pizza" and "Pigganelli Recreation
and Rehab Center." The brothers hang balloons and a banner outside: "Xbox
tournament every Wednesday! Sign up today! FREE CAKE!"

The overall theme is this: shortcuts can have too high a price.

After you have listed your scene summaries like this, put abbreviations of
your scenes in a line-of-action chart, so you can see if each line of action is
well developed. Here, for example, is the chart for *The Three Little Pigs*. The
X's indicate scenes that do double duty in other lines of action, and the bold
horizontal lines indicate act breaks. The main character in each scene has
the abbreviated scene description in his box.

## Trailer

One way to test your scenario is to write a trailer – the most important
marketing tool for a film. An effective trailer successfully communicates
the experience of the film. It plays in theaters several weeks before the
film opens and on television a week before. A trailer is typically created
by postproduction editors, who draw the material for the trailer from
the same footage shot for the film itself. They may add graphics (like text
panels: "Coming This Summer"), special effects (like a full-screen explosion designed just for the trailer), or music and sound effects (like the
slam-of-metal sound we might hear when the title comes up for a movie
like *T2*). They generally use voice-over narration, taken either directly
from the dialogue tracks ("Help me, Obi-Wan. You're my only hope.") or

| Lou$_1$ | Lou$_2$ | Frankie | Rocco |
|---|---|---|---|
| Talks to his brothers about changing their futures | | X | X |
| The brothers pool their resources | | X | X |
| | | Frankie builds his house | |
| | | | Rocco builds his house |
| Lou builds his house | | | |
| Lou uses cheap shingles and dreams of his "windfall" | | | |
| | | The wolf threatens Frankie | |
| | | Frankie's house comes down | |
| | | Frankie's roof falls on the wolf's foot | |
| | | X | The wolf threatens Rocco |
| | | X | Rocco's house comes down |
| | | X | Rocco's roof falls on the wolf's foot |
| Frankie and Rocco arrive at Lou's | | X | X |
| X | Wolf threatens Lou | X | X |

| Lou₁ | Lou₂ | Frankie | Rocco |
|---|---|---|---|
| X | Wolf climbs on roof | X | X |
| X | Lou starts a fire in the fireplace | X | X |
| X | Wolf sets Lou's roof on fire | X | X |
| Lou runs off for something | X | X | X |
| Lou retrieves insurance forms | X | | |
| The roof implodes and crashes down | X | X | X |
| Neighbor arrives at Lou's home, and Lou flees | X | X | X |
| | | Frankie and Rocco rush to the door | X |
| | X | Frankie offers cake to wolf | X |
| | Wolf is arrested | X | X |
| In prison, Lou and the wolf have lost their futures | X | | |
| | | Frankie and Rocco put a solid roof on Lou's house, and Frankie opens his pizza shop and Rocco his center | X |

**Monsters, Inc., 2001**

from an entirely separate vocal recording ("Star Wars: The story of a boy, a girl, and the universe.").

Sometimes teasers are used instead of trailers. The main difference between a trailer and a teaser is that the former is usually drawn from the actual footage of the film itself while the latter is not. In fact, teasers are usually made long before a film is in postproduction and sometimes even before a single frame of the actual film has been shot. PIXAR successfully uses teasers to promote its films months before the films themselves are finished. In the very first teaser for *Monsters, Inc.,* two monsters employed by the company that scares children emerge together from a closet but discover an empty room and bicker about which one of them read their assignment schedule wrong. (In the film, every professional child-scarer enters the human world solo, assisted by a handler who remains at headquarters.) It is delightful footage that never appears in the actual film. Even though the teaser wasn't taken from the film footage, it was memorable and effective because it did its job well: it successfully communicated the experience of the film.

As a screenwriter, it is unlikely that you will be directly involved in creating a trailer for your own film, but writing one will help you (1) practice being concise in your thinking and writing, (2) find weak elements in your story while you can still correct them, and (3) fine-tune the tone and emotional resonance of your story. If you can't convey the tone and experience of your film in a trailer, your story needs polishing.

Here is a way to go about creating a script for your trailer. Select several scenes from your synopsis, and from each of these glean interesting bits of your story. Arrange the bits into a script (using appropriate devices like narration) with a run time of about two minutes (which means the script should be between two and three pages long). A good trailer (1) quickly gets to the main action, (2) builds to a major turning point when it looks as if the main character won't be able to accomplish his aim, then (3) offers hope that the main character will be able to accomplish his aim but doesn't reveal whether or not he does. Structure your trailer as follows:

- In the first few seconds, introduce the main character and action.
- In the first 80 seconds, develop the action and build to a main turning point, when it looks as if the main character won't be able to accomplish his aim.
- In the last 40 seconds, pose questions, evoke emotions, and suggest meaningful solutions but don't directly reveal them.
- In the last few seconds, show a memorable moment.

Let's look at an example. Watch this short trailer (52 seconds) on YouTube: *Harry Potter Order of the Phoenix* movie trailer. See if you can find in the trailer the four structural parts listed above. Here is a script for the trailer:[5]

**Harry Potter and the Order of the Phoenix, 2007**

Opening Shot: Warner Brothers logo flying through clouds. Clouds part to skyline nighttime shot of London, and then sweeping shot pans down and dissolves to shot of Sirius sitting at Grimmauld Place.

Sirius Black at Grimmauld Place: Fourteen years ago, Voldemort had huge numbers at his command.

Quick shots of hooded, gold-masked Death Eater.

Shot of Professor Dumbledore standing before fully assembled Wizengamot.

Albus Dumbledore: The evidence the Dark Lord's returned is incontrovertible.

Shots of exploding proclamations (educational decrees) on the Great Hall wall.

Full Screen words: On July 13.

Shot of Harry Potter standing in Snape's office.

Voice-over of Professor Severus Snape: You won't last two seconds if he invades your mind.

Quick shots are shown of Hermione in Forbidden Forest, Shot of Ron, Ginny, DA in background.

In the Room of Requirement, Voldemort in grave-yard, wand drawn from dueling (probable flashback to *Goblet of Fire*), then back to shot of Harry in Snape's office.

Harry Potter: I'm not weak!

Professor Severus Snape: Then prove it!

Full Screen Shot with words: A New Order Begins.

Shot of Harry sitting in kitchen of Grimmauld place, with Fred, George, Hermione present.

Harry Potter: If Voldemort's building up an army, then I want to fight.

Series of quick shots:

Proclamation of Educational Decree exploding off of wall.

Gold-masked Death Eater.

Ron ducking.

Harry falling.

Umbridge standing before swing clock pendulum.

Harry kissing Cho.

Umbridge pointing wand.

Harry flinging back toward wall.

Order of the Phoenix flying on brooms over River Thames past a large ship.

Bellatrix Lestrange firing her wand.

Hallway into a darkened room as it gets closer to Snape pointing wand at Harry.

Harry falling back into wall in Snape's office in pain.

Pink-suited Umbridge running up the aisle among students, clearly panicked.

Voldemort emerging from the mist.

Trio in woods, falling back as if afraid.

Order flying on brooms past the Parliament building at night in London.

Screen goes black with only the sound of a clock's gong, then...

Full Screen words slowly appear: Harry Potter and the Order of the Phoenix.

Closeup shot of Harry Potter zooming toward camera full on, flying on broom.

Full Screen words over cloudy background: July 13, 2007.

Before you write a script for your trailer, watch lots of trailers online and make your own observations. If you find that you are having difficulty coming up with your story's "trailer moments," go back and rework your scenario.

## Audience Test

When your scenario draft is completed, audience test it. Email it to friends (without your statement of the theme), and simply ask them to respond to statements similar to those you presented for your synopsis. Again, use a five-point scale. If you get strong disagreements, study them, make your revisions, and test again.

### As the story began:

1. I began to care about the main character
2. I had some idea of what the main character was trying to do
3. I had an idea of how the main character might develop
4. I understood how the other characters were impeding or helping the main character

### As the story developed:

5. I cared more about the characters
6. I better understood the nature, difficulty, and importance of what the characters were trying to do
7. I had a better idea of how the characters were developing
8. Each scene left me wondering what the characters would do next
9. What the characters did in each scene grew out of what they did in earlier scenes
10. I noticed several major turning points in what the characters were trying to do
11. I understood who the main character was in each scene

### As the story ended:

12. I didn't feel manipulated
13. I cared about the characters significantly more than I did in the beginning
14. I understood how the characters completed or abandoned their pursuits
15. I believe the characters finally came to insights or decisive choices

16. I value the insights or decisive choices the characters came to
17. I can state a theme that summarizes the insights or decisive choices the characters came to:

_____

## The Next Chapter

In these last three chapters, you have summarized your script and novel, first as a one-sentence pitch, then a five- or six-page synopsis, and finally a fifteen- to twenty-page scenario. At last, it is time to start expanding your summaries, filling them out first as a script and then as a novel.

## Student Writing Group

### Week Six

1. Read the introduction to this chapter and the assignments for weeks six and seven. Write your questions; then read the chapter, and write your answers.

> *Don't we need to develop the other lines of action early on for the sake of the main one? Why are we developing them now when I needed them when I was developing the main line of action?* The main line of action needs the bulk of my focus first, because the rest of the lines of action must support or complicate the main one. It's okay to have inklings of the other lines of action, so long as I'm focusing on the main one first.

2. Write down the lines of action in the movie you wrote key scenes for in the last chapter. For each line of action, write one sentence that includes the action, the initial characterization, and the final characterization.

> Speed Racer, a talented but naïve racer, purifies the sport of racing and learns to rely on his own goodness and the goodness of his friends and family.
>
> Racer X, who has become a bitter, hardened, justice-driven racer, finally achieves his goal of changing the sport of racing and learns that it is not foolhardy to have hope in the future.
>
> Pops, a stubborn, opinionated, somewhat narrow-minded father, is trying to figure out how to deal with his son, Speed, and learns that to be what his son needs most he has to recognize that his opinions are not always right.

3. Write down the main line of action and the opposing and supporting lines of action for the film novel you are writing. For each line of action,

write one sentence that includes the action, the initial characterization, and the final characterization.

Sam₁: Sam, a cocky, headstrong fourteen-year-old boy, tries to rescue his kidnapped sister from a tribe of modern Aztec restorationists and learns that sacrifice isn't just giving something up to help someone – it is opening the way for others to do what you can't.

Temkai: Temkai, a dutiful prince, tries to help his father restore the earth, but when he discovers his father's pride has drawn him away from the path of truth, the prince sees that truly honoring his father is only possible by disobeying him.

Lyman: Lyman Sutter, a family man and respected leader in the community, tries to make his son, Sam, grow up by being more of a manager than a father, but learns, when he almost loses Sam, that he was missing out on the best parts of family life and fatherhood by not recognizing and loving the man Sam is becoming.

Sam₂: Sam, who resents being managed and pushed by his father to become more like him, takes on hardships to prove himself and learns to appreciate his father and the man that he himself is becoming.

Charlotte: Charlotte, a devout young woman training to be a nurse, tries to help establish a caring religious community and discovers she can learn much from her mysterious captors about faith, love, and sacrifice.

Ashkea: Ashkea, a devoted Aztec princess who loves her father but believes he has lost his way, tries to persuade him with love and wisdom that restoring some ancient rituals will have too high a price and discovers that only a great sacrifice will penetrate her father's pride.

Russian: Russian, a grizzled, savvy loner and former CIA agent trying to find peace in solitude, initially regrets acting on instinct to protect a defenseless kid who won't go away, but discovers that peace is possible only when you have people to love – even though you may lose them. (Russian does not appear in the Act 1 excerpt below, but his line of action is vital to moving Sam's forward in the rest of the story.)

4. Write down the theme of your film novel. Make sure it fits with the final characterizations in your lines of action, each final characterization bringing out something that complements or contrasts with the theme. Rewrite the theme if necessary.

New theme: A loving sacrifice is more powerful than any victory.

*Week Seven*

1. Write a scenario for your script and novel by doing the following: (a) Write a one-paragraph summary of each scene in your opposing and supporting lines of action, and weave these summaries into the scene summaries for your main line of action. Indicate in brackets, at the beginning of each scene summary, which lines of action the scene is a part of. Make sure each scene moves the lines of action it is a part of either forward or backward. For each line of action, include summaries of one or two scenes with major turning points. Some of these major turning points should occur near the main act breaks you established for your main line of action. Use bold horizontal lines to indicate act breaks. (b) Write a one-sentence statement of the theme at the end.

Again, because of publishing constraints, we'll include just the first act of the scenario.

[Ashkea, Temkai] We see a starlit sky. Ashkea recounts in voice-over what her people believe and how the Apocalypse came about: "There's a certain way the universe works: the Gods and Man share responsibility for preserving order and balance." Aztec figures appear like constellations in the sky, animating her tale. The figures "Gods" and "Man" join hands. She continues: "In the last days of the fifth sun, Man thought he had learned all that was needful. He planted pride in his heart. He let go of God's hand. His pride grew like a tangled vine; its fruits fell like fire until all the earth burned." Smoke rolls. Transition to live slow motion: horses' hooves beat up dust. She continues: "The Gods whispered to my father, a scholar of the ancient codes. He must restore abandoned rituals and thus restore the earth. My brother, Temkai, will be an emissary, to find 'waxing water.' Earth's renewal will begin at Crooked Sky." Ashkea watches from a high cliff as three riders gallop away. It is early dawn; a full moon still hangs in the morning sky. She says she prays for her brother's safe return, and every day she implores the Gods: "Please, don't let my father let go of your hand."

[Sam$_1$, Charlotte] It is spring 2022 in a highly organized, high-fenced Christian community named 'Liberty' in the western states region. Sam Sutter shirks his chores to play poker with three buddies, hiding in a fort lookout. Meanwhile, his sister Charlotte looks for him. Sam wins hand after hand and brags to his friends that luck has chosen him – he'd even be lucky out *there* with the "rogueys." He points to the world beyond their fences. Nathan says he can only play one more hand. Then he has to bring the generator up to the dairy for Mr. Thompson. Sam says that would only take *him* fifteen minutes. Nathan has plenty of time! The boys hear Charlotte and freeze, eager not to be found. Mike whispers that Charlotte has gotten "hot." Angered, Sam swings at him. Nathan intercedes, and the boys are silent until she is gone. Sam glares at Mike. Glancing beyond the fence, Sam sees a figure approach in grave distress, then stumble and fall. He drops his cards and runs for Charlotte.

[Charlotte, Lyman] Charlotte, a junior nurse, helps resuscitate the man. Lyman Sutter watches with friend Jay, who says he almost hopes the man is from the Tacoma group. They haven't heard from Daniels in weeks. The man manages to say they were attacked "… at Mercy Falls … please help us!"

[$Sam_1$, $Sam_2$, Charlotte, Lyman] Lyman prepares a team to bring the refugees in. Knowing Charlotte plans to go with the rescuers, Sam tries to persuade Lyman to let him go in her stead. He's old enough, and he's concerned about her safety out there. Lyman refuses – they need Charlotte's skills. Sam angrily suggests Lyman will be "too busy saving the world" to protect her. Lyman snaps: "It's a good thing you're a lucky ace – a man who can't listen to anyone else is gonna need all the luck he can get!" Sam leaves.

[$Sam_1$, $Sam_2$, Charlotte, Lyman] The Hawkins brothers pass by. Winking, they assure Sam they'll keep a good eye on his sister. Provoked, Sam decides to do whatever it takes to be part of the rescue team. He returns submissively and pleads with Lyman, agreeing to do anything he asks. Lyman and Ellie (Sam's mother) agree it might be a good experience – he's too big for his britches. Ellie gives him an emergency whistle on a lanyard and demonstrates three sharp blows – "so Dad will know it's you." Sam is embarrassed when heads turn. Ellie instructs him: "Don't take that off."

[$Sam_1$] Sam is sandwiched between two heavyset people driving the horse-drawn, retrofitted medical trailer to Mercy Falls. When the Hawkins boys ride up and make fun of the whistle from Sam's mommy, he points out that *some* mothers *want* their sons to come home. They leave.

[$Sam_1$, $Sam_2$, Charlotte, Lyman] Arriving at Mercy Falls, Sam is awed by his first glimpse of a waterfall. He tries to hide his shock at seeing the wounded refugees. The team quickly sets up a modest, organized field hospital. Charlotte is capable and compassionate; they move the wounded into the tent. Lyman emphasizes to all: "NO ONE sets foot outside camp alone!" Sam is told to gather firewood and is glad to be busy. He overhears men say they found Captain Daniels; he's dead. Sam hastens nearer to Charlotte. She subdues a crying child and directs Sam to fetch a "morphiloxadil suspension." He watches her treat the child and soothe her into a relaxed sleep.

[Sam$_2$, Lyman] Hoping for a more "important" job, Sam enters his father's tent uninvited. He overhears the men say that they know nothing of the refugees' attackers. Sam offers to scout around; he's good at finding things. Lyman says no; Sam already has a job. "Just do it well."

[Sam$_1$, Charlotte] Charlotte joins Sam at a fire. He feels better with her nearby. Charlotte asks what he thinks of the world "outside of Liberty." Sam says it's no big deal; like everything else, being *safe* is all about being *smart*. Charlotte assures him: "It's no accident that we're here helping these people right now. You are always protected and safe when you are doing God's will." Sam asks: "But ... what if it isn't God's will to keep you safe?" Before she can speak, Lyman calls them to bed.

[Sam$_1$, Charlotte] In the morning, Charlotte asks Sam to go to the falls with her to wash up. Sleepy, he tells her to catch up to her friends; he just heard them leave. "Fine," she says, "but if they're not there, I'll come back for you." Still half asleep, he agrees.

[Temkai] Temkai and his band hide a distance away and watch the camp.

[Charlotte] Charlotte arrives at the falls and doesn't see her friends but is enchanted by the waterfall. She drops her knapsack and slips off her shoes to dip her feet in the pond for a moment. Just as she turns back, she hears a woman call for help from the trees: "Please, my foot is stuck!" Supposing she is a refugee, Charlotte goes to help.

[Sam$_1$, Sam$_2$, Charlotte, Lyman] Lyman gives Sam a breakfast plate. As he eats, his whistle clinks against his plate. He removes it and drops it nearby. Sam absently returns the greeting of Charlotte's two friends before it hits him that Charlotte must be alone. Then, alarmed, Sam abandons his plate to run to her. Lyman doesn't notice Sam go.

[Temkai] As Charlotte follows the voice, Temkai goes to her knapsack and ID to confirm her birth date: she is a "water sign." He signals to Riley.

[Charlotte, Temkai] Charlotte reaches the woman, only to find she has been tricked: the supposed refugee is Jaz, one of Temkai's band. Charlotte bolts, but is captured by Temkai. She reaches for her whistle, but Jaz rips it off and throws it down.

[Sam$_1$, Charlotte, Temkai] Sam arrives to see Charlotte wrestled out of view. She calls to Sam and is gagged. Running, Sam sees her abductors escape on horseback. He fumbles for his whistle, then remembers in horror that he took it off. He runs and spots her whistle by the pond. He snatches it up and makes three sharp blows, running after the horses to track their trail.

[Sam$_2$, Lyman] The three sharp blows are heard again, but in camp, the sound is faint. Finally, Lyman hears it and shouts, "Sam!"

Theme: Sacrifice is more powerful than any victory.

2. Abbreviate your scene summaries and put them in a scenario chart. Make sure each line of action is well developed. Revise if necessary.

   Here is the chart for the above scenes. We didn't include Russian's line of action because he doesn't appear until the second act.

3. Write a two-minute trailer for your film. If you don't have the makings of an engaging trailer, revise your scenario.

   Our trailer script is online at www.greatcinemanow.com/filmnovelist.

4. Audience test your scenario, emailing at least six people. Summarize your experience with your respondents, and explain how this feedback can help you.

   The results of our audience test are online.

| | Sam₁ | Charlotte | Lyman | Ashkea | Temkai | Sam₂ |
|---|---|---|---|---|---|---|
| | | | | V.O about balance, apocalypse, and man 'letting go of God's hand' Her father's mandate to renew earth | X | |
| | Sam dodges chores and wins at poker Charlotte looks for Sam; he defends her honor Sam sees an approaching refugee | X | | | | |
| | | Charlotte nurses the injured man and learns there are more injured | X | | | |
| | X | X | Lyman prepares a rescue team Charlotte is going; Sam wants to go to protect her and is forbidden | | | X |

| Sam$_1$ | Charlotte | Lyman | Ashkea | Temkai | Sam$_2$ |
|---|---|---|---|---|---|
| Provoked by the Hawkins brothers, Sam submits and begs Lyman to let him go. Ellie gives him an emergency whistle | X | X | | | X |
| Sam is teased about whistle; he rebuffs well | | | | | |
| Sam sees his first waterfall He is rattled by suffering of the refugees and learns their captain is dead. Sam obeys Lyman. Sam watches Charlotte administer aid | X | X | | | X |
| | | Sam wants a more important job; offers to scout and is denied. | | | X |

| Sam₁ | Charlotte | Lyman | Ashkea | Temkai | Sam₂ |
|---|---|---|---|---|---|
| Sam does his job (tends fires) and discusses safety and God's will with Charlotte | X | | | | |
| X | Charlotte asks Sam to go with her to wash up; he tells her to try her friends first, then him | | | | |
| | | | | Temkai and his band, hidden in the hills, watch the camp below | |
| | Charlotte's friends aren't at the falls; she turns back but hears a woman in distress | | | | |
| X | Sam realizes Charlotte never came back and bolts to the falls, disobeying Lyman | X | | | X |

| Sam₁ | Charlotte | Lyman | Ashkea | Temkai | Sam₂ |
|---|---|---|---|---|---|
| | | | | Temkai checks Charlotte's ID to confirm she is the one | |
| | Charlotte sees she was tricked Temkai seizes her, Jaz tears off her whistle | | | X | |
| Sam arrives to see abduction; fumbles for his missing whistle but finds hers; blows and runs in pursuit | X | | | X | |
| | | Lyman hears the distant whistle and reacts | | | X |

— 117 —

# Stage Three: Expanding

# Script

In this chapter, which will take you three weeks to complete, you will turn your scenario into a script in two steps. First, you will replace your scene summaries with scene description and summarized dialogue and voice-over. Then you will turn your summarized dialogue and voice-over into actual lines. Once you get the scene description in place, the dialogue and voice-over will come naturally.

### Week Eight

1. Read the introduction to this chapter and the assignments for weeks eight through ten. Write your questions; then read the chapter, and write your answers.
2. Find a film script scene you like online, and write it down. Under the slug line, write what the main character in the scene is trying to do. Then use slashes to mark the turning points that divide the scene into smaller units—the beats.
3. Rewrite your scenario as a "beat script"—a script with scene description and summarized dialogue and voice-over laid out in beats. After each slug line, state the action of the main character in the scene.

### Week Nine

1. In the first half of your script, replace the summarized dialogue and voice-over with actual dialogue and voice-over.

### Week Ten

1. In the second half of your script, replace the summarized dialogue and voice-over with actual dialogue and voice-over.
2. Audience test your draft, and explain how this feedback can help you.

### Glossary

| | |
|---|---|
| **slug line** | A header for a scene, indicating where and when the scene takes place—like "EXT. HOUSE—DAY" |
| **beats** | The basic units of the main action in a scene, which are separated by small turning points |
| **beat script** | A script with scene description and summarized dialogue and voice-over laid out in beats |
| **full scenes** | Scenes that have turning points |
| **half scenes** | Scenes that don't have turning points (used in montage sequences) |
| **direct statement** | An explicit statement of a character's thoughts, feelings, or intentions |
| **indirect statement** | An implicit statement of a character's thoughts, feelings, or intentions |

## Beats

Major turning points divide stories into acts, and lesser turning points divide acts into scenes. The smallest turning points divide scenes into what are called beats. Beats convey the developing action of a main character in a scene. A beat ends when the dynamics of a scene have significantly changed for the character—whenever readers find themselves asking, "Now what's he going to do? How's he going to act or react to what has just happened?" Here is the basic pattern for marking beats:

/John does this, but then this happens.

/So he adapts what he is doing like this, but this happens.

/So he adapts and ends up doing this.

Turning points function in scenes just like turning points in lines of action in a film: they indicate where the potentialities for action change. Scenes can be like "separate little film[s],"[1] writes filmmaker Jean Renoir.

**To Kill a Mockingbird, 1962**

Here is a scene from *To Kill a Mockingbird*, which I have summarized and divided into six beats. The main character is Scout, who is trying to protect her father. New beats begin when we wonder what Scout will do next. After the slug line, I've put in brackets Scout's main action in the scene.

EXT. JAIL—NIGHT

[Scout is trying to protect her father.]

/Scout, with her brother and friend, spot Atticus sitting in a chair on the porch of the city jail, watching over the black man he is defending. Then they see noisy cars come into view and men with rifles piling out and moving toward the jail.

/Scout and the other children rush up between the men to Atticus to protect him. Mr. Cunningham and the other men demand that the children leave. Scout's brother refuses, and the men start to force him to leave.

/Scout starts kicking the men. Then she recognizes Mr. Cunningham.

/Scout greets Mr. Cunningham and talks about how she goes to school with his boy. He and the other men seem uncomfortable.

/She turns to her father and apologizes. Mr. Cunningham defends her and tells the men to leave.

/Scout and the other children leave, and the camera lingers on a distant shot of Atticus again sitting in front of the jail.

Notice that the camera lingers on the jail, giving viewers time to think about what has just happened. Writers can also linger on a scene, Sibyl Johnston explains, by adding "brief descriptions of the characters or setting" that "create pauses" in the action. "These breathing spaces," she continues, "will allow time for subterranean emotions to resonate and register."[2] What happens in this scene is deeply significant—it is a high point of the film—and we as viewers need time to reflect on it, both when we read the scene and when we watch it on film.

Notice also that Scout's movements change in the scene. She is motionless for the first beat, moving for the second, kicking for the third, still for the fourth, turning to her father for the fifth, and moving for the sixth. The beat changes occur when Scout starts, stops, or changes direction. When a scene is well written, beat changes are reinforced by changes in the movement of the main character in the scene. Sometimes the changes are abrupt—the character stops moving for a moment at the end of one beat and immediately starts moving again at the beginning of the next. Sometimes the changes are not abrupt—the character stops moving at the end of one beat, is still for another beat, and then starts moving again at the beginning of the next beat.

The above scene is a so-called full scene—one with turning points. Scenes without turning points are called half scenes, and they simply state what a character does before encountering a turning point. "John starts to open the door, but it is locked" is the action of a full scene. "John opens the door" is the action of a half scene.

Half scenes aren't engaging by themselves but may become so when they are part of a montage sequence of half scenes. To make montage sequences engaging, writers leave gaps in the action between the half scenes. The gaps in the action are simply jumps in time that move readers more quickly toward the end of an action and engage them in imagining not only what the overall action is but what turning points occurred between the half scenes. By leaving gaps in the action of a story, writers can tell more of the story in a shorter time and can tell stories that otherwise couldn't be told. As Leitch writes, "Feature-length films, with rare exceptions, can present tellable stories only by cutting from shot to shot, encouraging the audience to supply the logically necessary connections."[3]

Here is an example of a montage sequence of half scenes, with our friend John as the main character. Notice how readers have to guess what John is trying to do and what happens between the half scenes.

```
MONTAGE: /John eagerly opens the door. /He reads a
note on the table. /He lays on his bed curled up
in a ball.
```

Robert McKee believes that montage sequences should be avoided because they don't have turning points and are simply expository: "With few exceptions, montages are a lazy attempt to substitute decorative photography and editing for dramatization and are, therefore, to be avoided."[4] He has overlooked the fact that montages can engage viewers in inferring the overall action and the turning points in that action.


## Your Beat Script

To rewrite your scenario as a beat script, rewrite each summarized scene. Start by indicating the setting of the scene with a slug line that states where and when the scene occurs, using "EXT." for exterior and "INT." for interior—for example, "INT. HOUSE—NIGHT." Then figure out who the main character in the scene is. If the scene is in just one line of action, then the main character in the scene is the main character in that line of action. But if the scene is in two or more lines of action, then the main character is probably the one who changes the most in the scene. In the jail scene we looked at, Scout is the main character, because she changes the most.

Once you have figured out who the main character in the scene is, write down the action of that character in the scene as simply as you can—what is the character doing? The action of the character in the scene should be part of a line of action of the character in the script. (If a new character comes into the scene or a character in the scene leaves, you may have what the French would call a new scene and Americans would call a subscene. Either way, the action of the main character may change or the main character may even change. If you have a subscene, you will need to put in brackets the action of the main character of the subscene.)

Once you have indicated the action of the main character in the scene, expand the summary of the scene into beats made up of scene description and summarized dialogue and voice-over. The series of beats should end with a beat that accomplishes the action in the scene or abandons it. Write your beats from the perspective of the main character in the scene—write what that character is seeing and hearing and trying to do. Your task is simply to bring out the turning points in the action of the main character in the scene.

For an example of this process, let's create beats for a scene with our characters John and Martha. Say this is the scene summary:

> John calls Martha, hoping to take her to a movie, and Martha tells him she is quite tired. So John says he'll come over and fix dinner.

We could expand that summary like this:

```
INT. JOHN'S OFFICE—EVENING

[John is trying to arrange a date with Martha.]

/John calls Martha, asking her if she would like
to go to a movie they have talked about. But
Martha tells him she is quite tired.

/So John suggests that he go get a DVD. But she
says it was a hard day.

/So John says he'll come over and fix some dinner
and they can talk.
```

In this scene, Martha creates turning points for John. But John can also create turning points for himself by completing little actions that open up new possibilities for the next little actions. In general, turning points occur when a character is interrupted in trying to accomplish some task or when the character actually accomplishes the task and has to now decide what to do next. The following example shows a character creating turning points for himself by accomplishing little tasks that are part of a little line of action for the scene:

```
EXT. MARTHA'S APARTMENT—EVENING

[John is trying to apologize to Martha.]

/John pulls onto Martha's street, comes to a stop,
and sits in the car.

/He rehearses a few ways of bringing up the sub-
ject and tentatively settles on one.

/He gets out of the car and walks to the front of
the apartment and comes to a stop.

/He knocks for a while and then drops his hand.

/He softly makes his apology to the closed door.
```

So there are two ways of marking beat changes in a scene with a main character. To illustrate, say John is the main character in a scene. Then the following way of marking the beats is appropriate: An action of John followed by an action of Martha, her action creating suspense about what John will do next.

```
/ Action of John. Action of Martha.

/ Action of John.
```

The following is also appropriate: a completed action of John, creating suspense about what he will do next:

```
/ Action of John completed.

/ Action of John.
```

But the following isn't appropriate when John is the main character in the scene, since it shifts the focus onto Martha, making us wonder most what she will do next:

```
/ Action of Martha. Action of John.
```

The above examples show how to write beats for a full scene. To write beats for a montage sequence, rewrite your scenario summary as follows: first, write the word "MONTAGE" instead of a slug line; second, write down an overall action the main character or narrator is pursuing in the montage sequence; third, create a sequence of brief scenes for that action; finally, trim back the endings of these scenes so they become half scenes, leaving your readers to infer any turning points that might have occurred in the gaps between the half scenes. For example, you could turn the action of John asking Martha for a date into the following montage sequence:

```
MONTAGE

[John is trying to arrange a date with Martha]

/John gets in his car and calls Martha, asking
her if she would like to go to a movie they have
talked about. /Driving on the freeway, John sug-
gests that he go get a DVD. /Pulling onto Martha's
road, John says he'll warm up some dinner for her
and they can talk.
```

Notice how natural it is to start guessing what has happened between these half scenes.

## Writing Your Dialogue

After you have rewritten your scenario as a beat script, the next step is to replace the summarized dialogue and voice-over with actual dialogue and voice-over. You will be able to use some of the summarized dialogue - you won't need to write all of the actual dialogue from scratch.

One of the best ways to write the dialogue (for a scene with two speaking parts) is to improvise it with another person, while the two of you carry out the movements of the scene, moving and stopping and sitting and standing according to the beat descriptions in the scene. But you don't have to let the other person create any lines. Here is a way to avoid that. You take the part of the person who speaks first, and the other person, your friend, takes the other part. You improvise the first speech and have your friend write down what you say and where you pause. (Knowing where the pauses naturally occur will help you later fit description into the scene.) Then—and this is key—you switch parts and start the scene from the beginning again. Your friend now says the first speech, just as you said it and he wrote it, and you improvise the second speech, which he writes down. You again switch parts and start from the beginning. Each time the two of you say all of the lines already composed, and then you say the next lines. In this way, you improvise all of the dialogue, and your friend helps you by saying the lines you need to respond to. After a while, you won't need to start from

**Tobias Wolff**

the beginning, just far enough back to build up to the next line to be improvised.

Here, for example, is how this process might work if you had improvised the dialogue for Tobias Wolff's story "Say Yes," one of the suggested readings in the appendix:

> You: Let's say I am black and unattached and we meet and fall in love.

You switch parts and start over.

> Your friend: Let's say I am black and unattached and we meet and fall in love (pause).
> You: Look, (pause) this is stupid. If you were black you wouldn't be you (long pause). If you were black you wouldn't be you.

You switch parts and start over.

> You: Let's say I am black and unattached and we meet and fall in love (pause).

Your friend: Look, (pause) this is stupid. If you were black you wouldn't
be you (long pause). If you were black you wouldn't be you.
You: I know. But let's just say.

You switch parts again and start over.

Your friend: Let's say I am black and unattached and we meet and fall
in love (pause).
You: Look, (pause) this is stupid. If you were black you wouldn't be
you (long pause). If you were black you wouldn't be you.
Your friend: I know. But let's just say (long pause).
You: Say what?

You switch parts and start over.

You: Let's say I am black and unattached and we meet and fall in love
(pause).
Your friend: Look, (pause) this is stupid. If you were black you wouldn't
be you (long pause). If you were black you wouldn't be you.
You: I know. But let's just say (long pause).
Your friend: Say what?
You: That I am black, but still me, and we fall in love. Will you marry me?

In this way, you continue switching parts until you have improvised
dialogue for the whole scene. If you don't have a partner to work with, you
can use a digital recorder. Just turn it on, move according to the action
of the scene, and improvise a speech; then back up the recorder, listen to
it, and record the next speech. This won't be as effective as working with
someone else, but it can still help. Eventually, you will be able to improvise lines without the help of a recorder or anyone else. You will just need
to think hard about the beats in your scene, then "forget" them (but let
them affect you peripherally) and envision the characters and write what
they say, "allowing that [they] might surprise you,"[5] in the words of Sibyl
Johnston.

### Your Script with Dialogue

Once you have improvised dialogue for a scene, put it into script format. Then weave in the scene description and voice-over from your
beat script. Replace pauses in your improvised dialogue with some of
the description or voice-over. The above dialogue could be put into
script format, and description and voice-over from Wolff's story woven
in as follows:

INT. KITCHEN—NIGHT

            HER
    Let's say I am black and unat-
    tached and we meet and fall in
    love.

He glances over at her. She is watching him and
her eyes are bright.

            HIM
    Look,
       (taking   a   reasonable
       tone)
    this is stupid. If you were
    black you wouldn't be you.

          HIM (V.O.)
    I realized it was absolutely
    true. There was no possible way
    of arguing with the fact that
    she would not be herself if she
    were black.

            HIM
    If you were black you wouldn't
    be you.

            HER
    I know, but let's just say.

He takes a deep breath.

            HIM
    Say what?

            HER
    That I'm black, but still me,
    and we fall in love. Will you
    marry me?

Once the scenes in the script are written, start revising the dialogue. Replace any dialogue or voice-over that doesn't let readers infer something about what the characters or narrator are thinking, feeling, or trying to do. For example, replace "I'm angry!" with something like this: He slams his fist on the table and says, "Get out!" Trim out any dialogue or voice-over that doesn't help express the attitudes of the characters or the narrator. Cut commonplace exchanges such as "Hello," "Goodbye," or "How are you?" unless they implicitly convey something revealing about the characters. Cut "expository" dialogue—sentences put in the mouths of characters not because they would say them or because they reveal something about the characters, but because readers need to know some information. It is better to put such information in narration or to intersperse it a few words at a time in dialogue or description, trusting that readers will piece it all together.

Johnston explains that the dialogue in first drafts of stories—her own included—is often too much like transcribed speech, too literal and spelled out. Keep dialogue taut, she advises: include "just enough to suggest what is going on" with the characters.[6] It may be necessary to "cut a line of dialogue down to a word between the first and second drafts." Writing contemporary fiction, she explains, is a matter of "learning to suggest rather than go on at length,"[7] of being "concise and understated, suggestive of meaning rather than explicit."[8] Here, from her book, is a scene (in novel form) before the dialogue has been trimmed.

"I don't want to forget him."

"I can't forget him. I guess I understand your mother's reasons, though. After all, I keep a picture of him by my bed so that when I awake he'll be beside me."

"Yes, well …." Anne stumbles, flushed by Marie's comment. "Would you like something to drink?" She finishes leading her into the kitchen.

"Coffee, if you don't mind?"

"That's fine, it'll be a few minutes."

Anne watches Marie find her way to a seat and then sets about preparing the coffee. She turns on the kettle and grabs a mug from the shelf. "Is instant okay?" Silence. Anne hates uncomfortable silences but she doesn't know what to say as she prepares the coffee. Luckily enough, the silence doesn't last long.

"Did you tell your parents about tonight?" Marie asks.

"I told them that you were coming to visit and that we were having a girls' night out at Theresa's house. A sort of wake."

"What did they say?"

"Nothing really except that they think it's great that we are spending time together and that they hope we'll be able to help each other through today."

Here is the scene trimmed, leaving only dialogue that helps convey subtext.

"I don't want to forget him."

"I keep a picture of him by my bed."

"Yes, well …." Anne stumbles, flushed. "Would you like something to drink?"

"Coffee, if you don't mind?"

Anne turns on the kettle and grabs a mug from the shelf. "Is instant okay?"

Silence. Anne doesn't know what to say.

"Did you tell your parents about tonight?" Marie asks.

"Sort of."

"What did they say?"

"Nothing really. They think it's great we'll be able to help each other through today."

Notice how engaging the scene is now: it gets us started interpreting it as soon as we begin reading it.

After you have trimmed your dialogue, get a friend to read it with you, each of you taking a part. See if the lines flow, each line growing out of the possibilities suggested in the previous line. Revise if necessary.

## Audience Test

Once you have a draft of your script, audience test it. Since most people aren't used to reading scripts, read your script to them, or have an actor or a group of actors read it. Or you may want to record it being read with a webcam, post the recording, and ask friends to watch it. Once your friends have heard a reading of your script, ask them to answer the same questions you used to audience test your scenario. Revise accordingly.

## The Next Chapter

In this chapter, you have written a screenplay in two stages—with summarized speech and with actual speech. It the next chapter, you will turn your script into a film novel.

## Student Writing Group

### Week Eight

1. Read the introduction to this chapter and the assignments for weeks eight through ten. Write your questions; then read the chapter, and write your answers.

*What do you mean by breaking the scenes down into smaller units? What's smaller than a scene?* A unit smaller than a scene is a beat. Within each scene are miniature turning points that create beats. A beat occurs every time the main character in the scene has to make a choice because something in the scene has changed. Maybe the mood has shifted because of something someone has said, or a new character has entered the room uninvited, or maybe an alien warship has descended on a medieval city and has abducted the king, his servants, and his goldfish.

2. Find a film-script scene you like online, and write it down. Under the slug line, write what the main character in the scene is trying to do. Then use slashes to mark the turning points that divide the scene into smaller units—the beats.

Our film scene marked for beats is online.

3. Rewrite your scenario as a "beat script"—a script with scene description and summarized dialogue and voice-over laid out in beats. After each slug line, state the action of the main character in the scene.

Here are the opening scenes (after the montage sequence with Ashkea's voice-over). The rest of the beat script is online.

TITLE: WESTERN REGION OF THE ORIGINAL STATES, SPRING 2022

EXT. A TREE IN THE UNTAMED WILD AREA—MORNING

[The narrator is taking us to Charlotte.]

/Close-up on a small, blue butterfly at rest on a pale tree limb.

/It takes flight, and we follow its POV over a rough, dry, untamed landscape up to and over the high fence surrounding Liberty, which is strikingly manicured and orderly by comparison. It finds Charlotte and leaves us with her.

EXT. LIBERTY COMMUNITY—MORNING

[Charlotte is looking for her younger brother.]

/In a community bustling with activity, CHARLOTTE SUTTER (18) walks swiftly through town, smiling and greeting people. She smiles to see Mr. Boyd out and about and asks if his shoulder is feeling better. He says she's like magic!

/She steps into the LIBERTY BAKERY from a side door to see several cheerful women at work. One of them is her mother, ELLIE SUTTER (43), who happily greets her.

/Charlotte asks her mother if she's seen Sam since breakfast. Ellie chuckles, sighs, and quips, "What? He's not right where he should be? That's a first!"

/Charlotte exits to continue her search.

EXT. LIBERTY COMMUNITY FORT LOOKOUT—MORNING

[Sam is entertaining the guys and protecting his older sister.]

/SAM SUTTER (14) and his buddies (NATHAN, JAKE and MIKE) hide, play poker, eat, and make a mess as several small white butterflies flit around, unnoticed. Sam, an expert card handler, smiles and shuffles the deck, entertaining his friends. He says, "Watch this"—and makes sure they do. Sam notices that Jake, seated directly across from him and eating a sandwich, watches Sam's face instead of the cards.

/Sam asks, "What?" Jake giggles and chokes on an inhaled crumb and indicates to Sam to wait a moment.

/Sam stops and cocks his chin at Nathan, who sits on Sam's right with his back to the crawl hole. He lobs a candy into Sam's mouth and announces that makes three for three! Jake can talk now. Laughing, he says that his brother Jason wants him to find out if Charlotte likes him. Mike, at Sam's left, and Nathan howl with laughter and pass a tub of caramel popcorn.

/Sam is clear: "Sorry, not interested." Jake protests that Sam has to ask her—he can't know what Charlotte would say! Sam reminds him that he DOES know Jason and a handful of other guys with their eye on Charlotte. Sam says he is "the first line of defense"—no one dates his sister without his approval. Jake gives up and watches Sam deal.

## Week Nine

1. In the first half of your script, replace the summarized dialogue and voice-over with actual dialogue and voice-over.

Here are opening scenes.

TITLE: WESTERN REGION OF THE ORIGINAL STATES, SPRING 2022

EXT. A TREE IN THE UNTAMED WILD—MORNING

Close-up on a small, blue butterfly at rest on a pale tree limb. It takes flight, and we follow its POV over a rough, dry, untamed landscape. It nears a high fence made of split logs, with bark like the limb it just left. It hesitates, then flies over the tall fence into a developed community, which is strikingly manicured and orderly by comparison. It finds Charlotte and leaves us with her.

EXT. LIBERTY COMMUNITY—MORNING

Liberty bustles with activity. CHARLOTTE SUTTER (18), wearing medical scrubs and an ID lanyard, smiles and walks swiftly through town. She greets an older man with a sling.

> CHARLOTTE
> Mister Boyd! Is your shoulder feeling better?

> MR. BOYD
> (smiles, lifts his arm)
> You're like magic, Charlotte!

Charlotte continues, stepping into the LIBERTY BAKERY.

INT. LIBERTY BAKERY—MORNING

Charlotte's mother, ELLIE SUTTER (41), and four OTHER WOMEN cheerfully knead bread, flour dusting their faces and aprons.

> ELLIE
> Hello, honey!

> CHARLOTTE
> Hey, Mom! Have you seen Sam since breakfast?

>                    ELLIE
>              (chuckles, sighs)
>        You mean he's not right where
>        he should be? That's a first!

Charlotte exits and continues down the street.

EXT. LIBERTY FORT LOOKOUT—MORNING

SAM SUTTER (14) and buddies NATHAN, MIKE, and JAKE
hide, play poker, and make a mess. Sam smiles and
entertains his friends with his expert card-han-
dling skills. Several small white butterflies flit
around. JAKE, directly across from Sam, grins and
eats a sandwich.

>                     SAM
>              Watch this!

SAM entertains his friends with his shuffling
skills. MIKE, at Sam's left, and NATHAN, at right,
are impressed. Sam notices Jake is watching his
face, not his cards. Sam frowns.

>                 SAM (CONT'D)
>              What?

Jake giggles; he coughs on an inhaled crumb. He
holds up a finger to indicate *wait*. Sam stops and
cocks his chin at Nathan.

>                 SAM (CONT'D)
>              Hit me!

Nathan lobs a chocolate high; Sam moves into place
and catches it in his open mouth.

>                   NATHAN
>           That's three for three!

Nathan fist-pumps, eats a chocolate, and tosses
the foil wrapper. Jake can talk now, but he keeps
laughing as he tries.

>                    JAKE
>        Sam! My brother wants me to ask
>        you … um … Jason wants to know if
>        you think Charlotte likes him!

Nathan and Mike howl with laughter and dig into
caramel popcorn.

            SAM
      (deadpan, to Jake)
    Jason? Sorry. Not interested.

            JAKE
    At least ask her! You don't know
    what she'll say.

Jake pulls the popcorn away from Mike, who snatches
it back.

            MIKE
    C'mon, Sam! Just deal!

            SAM
      (still to Jake)
    But I DO know Jason—and Brock,
    and Kevin, and the guy with the
    goats…?

            NATHAN
    Elliott?

            SAM
      (points at Nathan, nods)
    Elliott.

Sam begins to deal the hand.

            SAM (CONT'D)
    Gentlemen, I am the first line
    of defense. No smelly guy is
    dating my sister without my
    approval.

Giving up, Jake sighs and watches Sam deal.

            JAKE
    I've got a bad feeling about
    this. Can I rub your lucky hat?

            SAM
    Nope. But you can rub Mike's
    head. Ante up!

                         MIKE
       What?!?

Jake reaches for Mike's head, and he dodges. Everyone
but Jake tosses some candy into the middle. Jake
turns his back to study the contents of an old
superhero lunchbox. They wait. He removes a candy,
throws it in, then tightly seals the box again.

Sam twists his cap around.

                     SAM (CONT'D)
           Okaaay. I'm in for two Nutty-
           Chews, three MasterCard thing-
           ies, and a twenty-fifteen Brett
           Favre!

Sam pushes the items into the middle.

                         MIKE
           No way! Is that Vikings?

                       NATHAN
           I thought Favre was Packers.

                        JAKE
       What's a Packer?

                        SAM
           Yeah, he was. Then it was
           the Jets, then Vikings, then
           Indianapolis Colts.

                        JAKE
                    (pensively)
           Where was Indianapolis?

                        SAM
           East coast someplace. It was
           famous for horse racing.

                       NATHAN
           Horse racing? You sure?

                        SAM
                 (tapping his noggin)
           Yes! Hello! The Colts?

They hear Charlotte calling for Sam. Game halts; they freeze.

                    CHARLOTTE (O.S.)
                     (exasperated)
                Sa-a-a-m!

Sam gestures for them to scoot quietly away from the hole with him; he leads. Jake peeks down the crawl hole then pops back.

                    JAKE
                (needlessly, to Sam)
                It's your sister!

All the boys aggressively shush him at once.

                    CHARLOTTE (CONT'D)
                Sam! Where are you?

Mike is nearest the crawl hole, and he peers down at Charlotte. Sam grabs the back of his shirt and jerks him back. Mike lands hard on his backside but gives Sam a wide grin.

                    MIKE
                Whoa, Dude! When did your
                sister get so hot?

Provoked, Sam silently cocks back to swing at Mike. Nathan, at Sam's right, grabs Sam's arm and scoldingly shushes them. Sam allows this intervention, but he gives Mike a stare-down.

                    CHARLOTTE
                Sa-a-a-a-m? Sam! Where is he?
                He never remembers!

The boys wait in silence, stifling laughter. One of the tiny white butterflies has landed on Sam's cap. Jake's eyes get wide, and he points at Sam's head like it's on fire. Sam looks behind him.

                    SAM
                (silently mouths)
                What?

The others point and mouth too: "Bug!" Sam smacks
the top of his cap, then takes it off to see the
bug. He drops it down the crawl hole; they watch
it flutter to the ground below.

> NATHAN
> (on knees, peering over
> wall)
> Okay—she's gone now.

They exhale and laugh; they ad-lib, "Phew! That
was close!"

Sam nudges them back to their spots.

> SAM
> We've got a game to finish! Mike,
> you gonna match me or what?

The guys reluctantly match, and the hand is called.

Sam slowly lays down three jacks, making "bomb"
sound effects with each one.

> SAM (CONT'D)
> As always, ladies, it's been a
> treat!

Sam tugs his hat on straight and scoops his winnings
into a knapsack while his friends gripe. Jake falls
back as if dead.

> SAM (CONT'D)
> Hey now—winning four in a row
> is harder than it looks!

Sam stands and closes his knapsack. His friends
sit, dejected. Mike, bored, throws popcorn kernels
at Jake's supine form.

> SAM (CONT'D)
> Or maybe I was just born lucky.
> You wouldn't hold that against
> a guy, would ya?

As Sam pulls the knapsack on, he sees something
far beyond the fence, and he stops laughing: A

distant, battered figure, approaching from the
west, struggles on foot, clearly in distress. He
stumbles and stays down.

Sam bolts down the fort ladder. His buddies ad-
lib: "Whoa! Hey—what's up?" Nathan and Mike hang
their heads down into the crawl hole.

>                     NATHAN
>           Sam! Where ya goin'?

>                     MIKE
>           Hey! Sorry I said your sister
>           is hot!!

Sam doesn't hear them; he is running, calling for
his sister.

>                     SAM
>           Chaa-aa-arlotte!

## Week Ten

1. In the second half of your script, replace the summarized dialogue and
   voice-over with actual dialogue and voice-over.

   Our script is online.

2. Audience test your draft, and explain how this feedback can help you.

   Our audience test is online.

# Novel

In the last chapter, you expanded your scenario into a script and polished your dialogue and voice-over. In this chapter, which will take you three weeks to cover, you will reformat your script as a novel and polish your scene description. You will work on the scene description in two stages—in first person and then in third person. The result will be a complete draft of a film novel in third person.

### Week Eleven

1. Read the introduction for this chapter and the assignments for weeks eleven through thirteen. Write your questions; then read the chapter, and write your answers.
2. Rewrite half of your script in novel format. Write in first-person past tense and from the point of view of the main character in each scene. Whenever there is a change in the main character, indicate who the new first-person character is by putting his name next to an "I," like this: *I, Bill, pushed my way through the crowd.*

### Week Twelve

1. Finish rewriting your script in novel format, still using first-person past tense.

### Week Thirteen

1. Rewrite your novel in third-person past tense, preserving the perspectives of the first-person characters.
2. Audience test your draft, and explain how this feedback can help you.

### Glossary

**point-of-view character**  The character from whose viewpoint a scene is described

**psychic distance**  The distance that the reader feels there is between himself and the events in the story—that is, whether the reader feels he is seeing events up close or from a distance

### Point of View

Scripts are always written in third person, present tense (*John opens the door*). But novels are most often written in third person, past tense (*John opened the door*). There are other options for novels—first person, past tense (*I opened the door*), even second person, past tense (*You opened the door*). And, of course, novels can be written in present tense like scripts. Altogether, there are six possible options for the voice and tense of novels. But there are good reasons for choosing the option of third person, past tense.

If we write in present tense, our narrator can be no smarter than he was during the story. So if we want a narrator who has learned something from experiencing the story, one who is guiding us through it, we need to write from the perspective of the narrator looking back—we need to use past tense. And if we write in first or second person, we can only have one point-of-view character throughout the novel. If we want to write from the point-of-view of different characters, we need to write in third person. (A third-person narrator can empathetically see from the point-of-view of one character after another.) So if we want a wise narrator and more than one point-of-view character, we need to write in third person, past tense.

A third-person narrator can sound like a first-person narrator by writing what is called indirect discourse, which is discourse that describes, in third person, what a subject would have perceived or said or thought in first person. There are two types of indirect discourse—free and not free. Indirect discourse is not free when the subject is stated—for example, *John noticed that his friend was gone*. Indirect discourse is free when the subject is not stated—for example, *His friend was gone*. A third-person narrator can write free indirect discourse (*His friend was gone*) by simply transforming first person discourse (*My friend is gone*) into third person. "Free indirect discourse [is] a subtle form of third person," Sibyl Johnston explains, "[that] allows the narrator to veer out to the very limit of the third person point of view, achieving an intimacy ordinarily reserved for the first person."[1] When we write free indirect discourse, we write as if we are seeing through the eyes of a character, but we can shift from one character to another. Free indirect discourse combines the immediacy of first person with the flexibility of third person.

The best way to understand free indirect discourse is to see a passage written in first person and then transformed into third. Take a simple first-person example from a student:

> I walked into this hotel room, and there was my tag-along sitting in a chair twiddling a fork.
> Mugwart looked up and said, "You're late."
> I sat down, casually crossed my legs, and just shook my head.

The first person narrator sees "this hotel room" and "my tag-along." That phrasing is preserved when the passage is rewritten in third-person:

> Warren walked into this hotel room, and there was his tag-along sitting in a chair twiddling a fork.
> Mugwart looked up and said, "You're late."
> Warren sat down, casually crossed his legs, and just shook his head.

The scene description is in third person, but it reflects the first-person point of view. What is described and how it is described indirectly convey something of what the character is thinking, feeling, and trying to do.

To understand the flexibility of free indirect discourse—the way it can shift from the point-of-view of one character to another—let's look at a more complex example. Scholars often turn to Flaubert for early examples of free indirect discourse. But there are much earlier examples in the Bible. "The Bible," scholar Adele Berlin writes, "excels in the technique of presenting many points of view and it is this, perhaps more than anything else, that lends drama to its narratives and makes its characters come alive."[2] Berlin discusses the story of Joseph and his brothers from the book of Genesis, showing how the narrator writes from the viewpoint of one character after another. By presenting diverse points of view, the narrator comes alive, not as a personality drawing our attention away from the characters, but as a generous storyteller, drawing us toward one character after another.

**de Ferrari's** *Joseph's coat Brought to Jacob*

Here is the opening of the story of Joseph, written in third person, with the phrases that reflect a first-person point of view in italics. Most of these phrases contain personal pronouns that express the relationship of the POV character to others in the scene.

[We begin with Jacob's point of view.] And Jacob dwelt in the land wherein *his father* was a stranger, in the land of Canaan. These are the generations of Jacob.

[Now the focus shifts to Joseph's viewpoint.] Joseph, being seventeen years old, was feeding the flock with *his brethren*; and the lad was with the sons of Bilhah, and with the sons of Zilpah, *his father's* wives: and Joseph brought unto *his father* their evil report.

[Back to Jacob, also called Israel.] Now Israel loved Joseph more than all *his children*, because he was the son of his old age: and he made him a coat of many colours.

[Back to Joseph] And when *his brethren* saw that their father loved him more than all *his brethren*, they hated him, and could not speak peaceably unto him. And Joseph dreamed a dream, and he told it *his brethren*: and they hated him yet the more. And he said unto them, "Hear, I pray you, this dream which I have dreamed: For, behold, we were binding sheaves in the field, and, lo, my sheaf arose, and also stood upright; and, behold, your sheaves stood round about, and made obeisance to my sheaf."

And *his brethren* said to him, "Shalt thou indeed reign over us? Or shalt thou indeed have dominion over us?" And they hated him yet the more for his dreams, and for his words.

And he dreamed yet another dream, and told it *his brethren*, and said, "Behold, I have dreamed a dream more: and, behold, the sun and the moon and the eleven stars made obeisance to me."

And he told it to *his father*, and to *his brethren*: and *his father* rebuked him, and said unto him, "What is this dream that thou hast dreamed? Shall I and thy mother and thy brethren indeed come to bow down ourselves to thee to the earth?"

And *his brethren* envied him; but *his father* observed the saying.

And *his brethren* went to feed their father's flock in Shechem.

[Back to Jacob.] And Israel said unto Joseph, "Do not thy brethren feed the flock in Shechem? Come, and I will send thee unto them."

And he said to him, "Here am I."

And he said to him, "Go, I pray thee, see whether it be well with thy brethren, and well with the flocks; and bring me word again." So he sent him out of the vale of Hebron, and he came to Shechem.

[Now we shift to the viewpoint of a stranger.] And a certain man found him, and, *behold*, he was wandering in the field: and the man asked him, saying, "What seekest thou?"

And he said, "I seek my brethren: tell me, I pray thee, where they feed their flocks."

And the man said, "They are departed hence; for I heard them say, Let us go to Dothan."

[Back to Joseph.] And Joseph went after *his brethren*, and found them in Dothan.

[Now we shift to the brothers' point of view.] And when they *saw him* afar off, even before he came near unto them, they conspired against him to slay him.

And they said one to another, "Behold, this dreamer cometh. Come now therefore, and let us slay him, and cast him into some pit, and we will say, 'Some evil beast hath devoured him': and we shall see what will become of his dreams."

[Now we shift to Reuben's viewpoint.] And Reuben *heard* it, and he delivered him out of their hands; and said, "Let us not kill him."

And Reuben said unto them, "Shed no blood, but cast him into this pit that is in the wilderness, and lay no hand upon him"; that he might rid him out of their hands, to deliver him to *his father* again.

[Back to Joseph.] And it came to pass, when Joseph was come unto *his brethren*, that they stript Joseph out of his coat, his coat of many colours that was on him.

And they took him, and cast him into a pit: and the pit was empty, there was no water in it.

When we write scenes from the viewpoint of characters, we invite our readers, in the words of Sibyl Johnston, "to enter [the] characters' lives, to feel through those characters."[3] "Staying close to [the point-of-view] character's physical senses," Johnston explains, invites the audience "to empathize with the character."[4] "It is an odd kind of empathy—good for the soul as well as the creative process."[5]

As writers, we need to make clear whose viewpoint each scene is being told from, so that readers don't feel, as Johnston says, "seriously disconcerted," "jerked around, betrayed, disrupted." She tells her writers that generally (1) "each scene should stick with one point-of-view" character,[6] (2) the point-of-view character should be established "early in the scene," and (3) point-of-view transitions should be made clear.[7] Stern suggests the following technique for changing point of view from one scene to another: end the first scene by describing the old point-of-view character, then start the next scene by describing the new point-of-view character and then his perceptions.[8]

## Writing Your Novel

Now turn each scene from your script into a *first-person* scene for your novel by following these steps: (1) Convert the slug line (like INT. HOUSE—NIGHT) into scene description that comes early in the scene. (2) Change the scene description and any voice-over into *first* person past tense (in order to bring out the point-of-view of the main character). Use a new paragraph for every new speaker. Use quotation marks for dialogue, and use speech tags like "he said" when they are necessary. We illustrate the process with a scene written by a student for the writer/director Lyman Dayton. Here is the scene in script form:

```
INT. BED AND BREAKFAST—NIGHT

Tim, in his pajamas, is leaving the bathroom late
one night. Eyes bleary, he has clearly just woken
up. He is heading back to bed when he stops at the
sound of his mom crying downstairs. Trying to be
as quiet as possible, Tim sneaks down the stairs.
Halfway down, he hits a creaky step and freezes,
wincing. After a few seconds and no lull in the
conversation downstairs, Tim continues until he
can hear clearly what is being said.

                    LANA
         I just don't know what I'm
         gonna do anymore!
```

> HAL
>
> It will be okay—I promise.

> LANA
>
> No, it won't. If I can't come up
> with this money soon, they are
> gonna shut me down!

> HAL
>
> You know I will never let
> that happen. Business will
> pick up.

> LANA
>
> I just don't know.

> HAL
>
> There's always ....

Hal reaches over and grabs Lana's hand affectionately.

> LANA
>
> You know I can't do that—
> not yet.

> HAL
>
> Just don't forget—I'm always
> here for you.

Tim is sitting horrified on the stairs. Feeling
terrible, he starts to go back up the stairs when
he hears Hal's police radio go off.

Tim turns back slightly to hear what the sheriff
is listening to on his radio. It is a 911-response
call about an emergency at the Brimhalls. Tim
hears his mom gasp, and he freezes.

> HAL (CONT'D)
>
> I have to go!

> LANA
>
> I'll come with you. Let me just
> grab Tim. Cody will need some-
> one ....

Tim starts when he hears his mom say his name,
runs up the stairs, and jumps in bed. We hear her

approaching. She stands in the doorway and takes
a deep breath before walking over.

                    LANA (CONT'D)
          Tim ....

Here is the scene in first person, past tense. Some of the scene description has been revised in this version. (For example, the line "Hal reaches over and grabs Lana's hand affectionately" has been cut since the narrator couldn't have seen that.)

I washed my hands and left the bathroom, blinking hard in the dark as I stumbled back to my room. Just as I was about to enter my bedroom, I heard a noise downstairs that made me pause. It was my mom, and I could hear her muffled sobs floating up from downstairs.

Turning, I made my way noiselessly to the stairs. Halfway down, I hit a creaky step and froze, wincing slightly. After a few seconds and no lull in the conversation, I continued heading down until I could clearly hear what was being said.

I could hear my mom speaking through her tears, "I just don't know what I'm gonna do anymore!"

Then I heard the voice of a man speaking softly, "It will be okay—I promise."

My mom choked up, "No, it won't. If I can't come up with this money soon, they are gonna shut me down!"

Hal responded more firmly this time, "You know I will never let that happen. Business will pick up."

I had to strain to hear what my mom said next. It was more muffled, like she had her head down on the table. "I just don't know."

Leaning forward on the banister, I heard Hal say softly, "There's always ...."

Then my mom spoke back clearly, "You know I can't do that—not yet."

Hal responded, "Just don't forget—I'm always here for you."

I sat down on the stairs and put my head in my hands. I sat there for a moment, then, using the railing for support, slowly made my way back up the stairs. Just as I reached the landing, I stopped again at the sound of Hal's police radio going off. I turned back slightly to hear what was being said and heard the dispatcher's voice through the static. All was quiet downstairs except for the static-filled voice asking for an immediate response to a 911 emergency. My mouth dropped as the dispatcher relayed the address twice—Cody's address.

When the voice stopped, I heard the screech of a chair being pushed back, and Hal said, "I have to go!"

When I heard my mom speak, her voice sounded choked. "I'll come with you. Let me just grab Tim. Cody will need someone ...."

I jumped at the sound of my name and turned back toward my room at the sound of footsteps approaching the stairs. Skipping across the room, I jumped in bed seconds before I heard footsteps right outside my door and the creak of the door being pushed open.

My mom's voice floated softly over, "Tim ...."

Once you have rewritten the scene in first person, rewrite it again in third person, preserving as much as possible of the first-person way of seeing things. The result is free indirect discourse. You will notice a few other revisions in this draft of the scene (e.g., several unnecessary speech tags have been removed).

Tim washed his hands and left the bathroom, blinking hard in the dark as he stumbled back to his room. Just as he was about to enter his room, he heard a noise downstairs. He stopped and turned. It was his mom, and he could hear her muffled sobs floating up from downstairs.

Turning, he made his way noiselessly to the stairs. Halfway down, he hit a creaky step and froze, wincing. After a few seconds and no lull in the conversation, he continued heading down until he could clearly hear what was being said.

He could hear his mom speaking through her tears, "I just don't know what I'm gonna do anymore."

Then he heard the voice of a man speaking softly, "It will be okay—I promise."

"No, it won't. If I can't come up with this money soon, they are gonna shut me down!"

"You know I will never let that happen. Business will pick up."

He had to strain to hear what his mom said next. It was more muffled, like she had her head down on the table. "I just don't know."

Leaning forward on the banister, he heard Hal say softly, "There's always ...."

"You know I can't do that—not yet."

"Just don't forget—I'm always here for you."

Tim sat down on the stairs and put his head in his hands. Then, using the railing for support, he slowly made his way back up the stairs. Just as he reached the landing, he stopped again at the sound of Hal's police radio going off.

He turned back to hear what was being said and heard the dispatcher's voice through the static. All was quiet downstairs except for the static-filled voice, "I need a response. This is a 911 emergency." His mouth dropped as the dispatcher relayed the address twice—Cody's address—142 Smith Drive.

A chair screeched as it was pushed back. "I have to go!"

"I'll come with you. Let me just grab Tim. Cody will need someone ...."

Tim jumped at the sound of his name and turned back toward his room at the sound of footsteps approaching the stairs. Hurrying across the room, he jumped in bed seconds before he heard footsteps right outside his door and the creak of the door being pushed open.

His mom's voice floated softly over, "Tim ...."

As you change your script into a novel, you may want to work first on all the scenes with the same main character, and then move on to scenes with other main characters, so that you can more easily create a coherent voice for each main character.

## Revising

Once you have moved your scenes from script to novel, go over your draft again, following these basic instructions:

First, use scene description—but not too much of it—throughout each scene. In a film novel, there can't be long stretches of dialogue or narration or interior monologue without any description. At every moment, the reader should be able to see what is happening in the scene. A good place to put description is where pauses occur in a conversation. Just cut any statement like "she paused" and replace it with description. But don't bog the scene down with too much description. Johnston explains why:

> When writing scenes, keep in mind the story's sense of time .... If you allow yourself to linger too long in descriptive detail ... the scene will seem to slow inappropriately. It will become frustrating to read. Unless you are trying for a special effect such as slow motion or intense, compressed action, you should not allow events to take significantly more or less time to describe than they would to observe.[9]

Second, state the characters' attitudes indirectly in the scene description (as you did in their speech in the last chapter). For example, instead of saying, "John was upset," say, "He shook his head and turned away." Go through each scene and mark all the direct statements of characters' attitudes, and then replace the direct statements of attitudes with indirect ones, so that readers can infer the attitudes. Here is a passage with several direct statements of characters' attitudes:

> Eliot, rather grumpy, glanced at the radio. Martha drove, self-absorbed, listening to the radio. Eliot disapproved. The morning sunlight fell on the wide-open ocean.
> Martha said, "I'm so glad you decided to come with me." She was delighted. "Saturday errands are so boring when I'm alone."

Here is the scene with the direct statements replaced with indirect ones (the passage comes from a student of Johnston):

> Eliot frowned and glanced at the radio. Martha drove, her eyes fixed on the road, humming along to "The Old Rugged Cross." Eliot sighed and cracked his knuckles. The morning sunlight fell on the wide-open ocean.
> "I'm so glad you decided to come with me." Martha leaned her head in his direction, a small smile on her lips. "Saturday errands are so boring when I'm alone."

Third, cut any scene description that doesn't help indirectly convey the attitudes of characters. Cut fancy speech tags, such as "he retorted with relish." Simple tags like "he said," "he asked," or "he answered" will do if the dialogue is well written. Cut speech tags altogether when it is obvious who is speaking—for example, when the paragraph begins with an action of the character who is about to speak. Cut words like "suddenly" or "immediately"—just have characters act suddenly or immediately.

Fourth, control shifts in psychic distance. John Gardner, writer and teacher, explains this concept:

> By psychic distance we mean the distance the reader feels between himself and the events in the story .... When psychic distance is great, we look at the scene as if from far away—our usual position in the traditional tale, remote in time and space, formal in presentation; as distance grows shorter—as the camera dollies in, if you will—we approach the normal ground of the yarn and short story or realistic novel. In good fiction, shifts in psychic distance are carefully controlled.[10]

It is much more important for a novelist than a scriptwriter to be able to control psychic distance. In a film, camera shots—close ups or wide shots or tracking shots—control the psychic distance, and directors don't like scriptwriters describing the camera setups. The directors will describe the shots themselves in a shooting script. But in a novel, the distance from which readers see scenes is part of the essential artistry of the book.

A good novelist will imitate a camera's action. (We will get into the camera's action in the next chapter. Understanding camera action is the best way to learn to control psychic distance in your writing.) When the beats change, so will "the camera"—it will cut in close or cut back or start or stop moving. It will be far away when the beat is less intense and close on faces when it is more intense, as in the following example: *The old man stepped out of the doorway and walked into the courtyard. From inside the house, someone called out his name. He stopped, then turned his head back and squinted as snow fell on his face.*

## Audience Test

Once you have a draft of your novel, you can audience test it using the statements you used for the scenario. Ask friends to read your novel, email them the statements and five-point scale, and get their feedback. If you get several strong disagreements, revise and audience test again.

## The Next Chapter

In these last two chapters, you have turned your scene summaries into a script and your script into a film novel. In the next chapter, you will video a scene from your script.

## Student Writing Group

### Week Eleven

1. Read the introduction for this chapter and the assignments for weeks eleven through thirteen. Write your questions; then read the chapter, and write your answers.

   *What is the benefit of writing a novel in first person before converting it to third person?* We are ultimately aiming to write free indirect discourse. We want our readers to personally experience what each character experiences, but we also want be able to switch points of view without a jarring effect. Writing a novel in first person sustains personal writing, and converting to third person allows for flexibility.

2. Rewrite half of your script in novel format. Write in first-person past tense and from the point of view of the main character in each scene.

Whenever there is a change in the main character, indicate who the new first-person character is by putting his name next to an "I," like this: *I, Bill, pushed my way through the crowd.*

Here are the opening scenes. The rest is online.

I, the butterfly, rested on the pale, grey bark of a young tree, folding and stretching my small, blue butterfly wings before taking off again and tracing a path over the dry soil, rough rocks, and untamed grass until I came to a tall fence made of split logs with the same soft bark as the tree I'd just left. I hesitated, but then continued over the fence into a neatly manicured, orderly community, where several people were busy doing the things people do. As I surveyed them from high above their heads, I was drawn to a fair-haired young woman making her way down the street. Her back was to me, and she wore a shade of blue much like mine. Her hair cascaded down her back. As I got closer, she turned in my direction to greet someone—finally revealing her face and her brilliant blue eyes.

I, Charlotte, walked swiftly down Main Street in Liberty, looking for Sam, greeting the people I passed. It was a busy Saturday morning. I smiled to see Mr. Boyd out and about, walking with his cane in his right hand and his left arm in a sling. I asked if his shoulder was feeling better. He gave me a big grin and said, "You're like magic, Charlotte!"

I stopped in at the bakery, where Mom was working and laughing with the others.

"Hello, honey!" Mom called, wiping her hands on her apron.

"Hey, Mom! Have you seen Sam since breakfast?"

Mom sighed and quipped, "You mean he's not right where he should be? That's a first!"

I said I'd keep looking.

While everyone else was busy being busy, I (Sam) and my buddies were hiding out in the fort lookout, sitting on the wood plank boardwalk and playing a little poker. I'm a pretty good card-handler, so I entertained them with my shuffling skills.

"Watch this," I instructed and showed them one of my best moves. Mike and Nathan were impressed, but Jake, sitting directly across from me, just grinned and ate his sandwich. He was watching my face, not my cards.

"What?" I asked. Jake giggled, then coughed as he inhaled a crumb. He held up a finger, indicating *wait*. I stopped shuffling and cocked my chin at Nathan. "Hit me."

Nathan lobbed a chocolate high in the air, and I moved to catch it in my mouth. "That's three for three!" Nathan pumped his fist. He laughed, ate one too, and tossed the wrapper aside.

Jake was ready to talk. "Sam, my brother wants me to ask you ...."
He couldn't stop laughing. "Um ... Jason wants to know if you think
Charlotte likes him."

Nathan and Mike howled with laughter and dug into the caramel
popcorn. I gave Jake a deadpan look. "Jason? Sorry. Not interested."

Jake protested, "At least ask her! You don't know what she'll
say!"

Jake pulled the popcorn away, and Mike snatched it back. "C'mon,
Sam! Just deal!"

"But I DO know Jason," I replied, "and Brock, and Kevin—and the
guy with the goats ...?"

"Elliott?" Nathan offered.

I pointed at Nathan and nodded once. "Elliott." I started dealing
again. "Gentlemen, I am the first line of defense. No smelly guy is dating
my sister without my approval."

## Week Twelve

1. Finish rewriting your script in novel format, still using first-person past
tense.

## Week Thirteen

1. Rewrite your novel in third-person past tense, preserving the perspectives of the first-person characters.

Here are opening scenes. The rest is online.

A butterfly rested on the pale, grey bark of a young tree, folding and
stretching its small, blue butterfly wings before taking off again and tracing a path over the dry soil, rough rocks, and untamed grass until it
came to a tall fence made of split logs with the same soft bark as the tree
it had just left. It hesitated, then continued over the fence into a neatly
manicured, orderly community, where several people were busy doing
the things people do. As the butterfly surveyed them from high above
their heads, it was drawn to a fair-haired young woman making her way
down the street. Her back was to it, and she wore a shade of blue much
like the butterfly's. Her hair cascaded down her back. As the butterfly got
closer, the young woman turned to greet someone—finally revealing her
face and her brilliant blue eyes.

Charlotte walked swiftly down Main Street in Liberty, looking for
Sam, greeting the people she passed. It was a busy Saturday morning. She

smiled to see Mr. Boyd out and about, walking with his cane in his right hand and his left arm in a sling. She asked if his shoulder was feeling better. He gave her a big grin and said, "You're like magic, Charlotte!"

She stopped in at the bakery, where her mother, Ellie Sutter, was working and laughing with the others.

"Hello, honey!" Ellie called, wiping her hands on her apron.

"Hey, Mom! Have you seen Sam since breakfast?"

Ellie sighed, "You mean he's not right where he should be? That's a first!"

Charlotte said she'd keep looking.

While everyone else was busy being busy, Sam and his buddies Nathan, Jake, and Mike were hiding out in the fort lookout, sitting on the wood plank boardwalk and playing a little poker. Sam entertained his friends with his shuffling skills.

"Watch this," he said and showed them one of his best moves. Mike and Nathan were watching closely, but Jake, sitting directly across from Sam, just grinned and ate his sandwich. He was watching Sam's face, not his cards.

"What?" Sam asked. Jake giggled, then coughed as he inhaled a crumb. He held up a hand, indicating *wait*. Sam stopped shuffling and cocked his chin at Nathan. "Hit me."

Nathan lobbed a chocolate high in the air, and Sam moved to catch it in his mouth. "That's three for three!" Nathan pumped his fist. He laughed, ate a chocolate, and tossed the wrapper aside.

Jake was ready to talk. "Sam, my brother wants me to ask you ...." He couldn't stop laughing. "Um ... Jason wants to know if you think Charlotte likes him."

Nathan and Mike howled with laughter and dug into the caramel popcorn. Sam gave Jake a deadpan look. "Jason? Sorry. Not interested."

Jake protested, "At least ask her! You don't know what she'll say!"

Jake pulled the popcorn away, and Mike snatched it back. "C'mon, Sam! Just deal!"

"But I DO know Jason," Sam said, "and Brock, and Kevin—and the guy with the goats ...?"

"Elliott?" Nathan said.

Sam pointed at Nathan and nodded once. "Elliott." He started dealing again. "Gentlemen, I am the first line of defense. No smelly guy is dating my sister without my approval."

Jake gave up and watched Sam deal. "I've got a bad feeling about this. Can I rub your lucky hat?"

"Nope." Sam tossed in his candy ante. "But you can rub Mike's head. Ante up!"

"What?" Mike squeaked, dodging Jake's reach.

Everyone but Jake tossed in a couple of pieces of candy. Jake turned around to study the contents of an old superhero lunchbox. The guys waited. Jake finally took out a candy, threw it in, then tightly resealed his lunchbox.

Sam twisted his cap around backwards and started the betting. "Okaaay, I'm in for two Nutty-chews, three MasterCard thingies, and a twenty-fifteen Bret Favre!" Sam pushed these to the middle.

"No way! Is that Vikings?" Mike asked.

Nathan answered, "I thought Favre was Packers."

"What's a Packer?" Jake asked.

"Yeah, he was," Sam said. "Then the Jets, then Vikings, then Indianapolis Colts."

Jake was thinking hard. "Where was Indianapolis?"

"East coast somewhere. It was famous for horse racing," Sam said.

Nathan looked at Sam sideways. "Horse racing? You sure?"

"Yes! Hello? The *Colts!*" Sam tapped a finger on his head.

That's when they heard Charlotte calling for Sam. They froze.

"Sa-a-a-am!" Charlotte called. Sam gestured for everyone to quietly scoot away from the crawl hole—in case she looked up. Jake peeked down the crawl hole, then popped back quick.

"Sam, it's your sister!" Jake needlessly informed them. They all shushed him at once.

"Sam, where are you?" Charlotte hollered. She sounded close. Mike was nearest the crawl hole, and he peered down into it. Sam grabbed the tail of his shirt and jerked him back, and he landed hard on his backside. He turned to Sam and grinned.

"Whoa, Dude! When did your sister get so hot?" Mike whispered. He didn't even see Sam's fist coming. Nathan caught Sam's arm. Sam let him stop it, but he glared at Mike.

"Sa-a-am?" Charlotte tried again. "Where is he? He never remembers!"

As they waited in silence, Jake's eyes went wide, and he started pointing at Sam's head like it was on fire. "What?" Sam mouthed. Sam looked behind him. Nathan and Mike were trying hard not to laugh. They pointed and mouthed, "Bug!"

Sam rolled his eyes. He reached up and swatted the top of his cap a couple of times, then removed it to survey the damage: a crushed little white butterfly. Sam dropped it down the crawl hole, and they watched it flutter to the ground.

Nathan was kneeling to peer over the half-wall. "Okay. She's gone now."

They all laughed—that was close! Sam nudged the guys back to their spots. "We've got a game to finish! Mike, you gonna match me or what?"

Everyone reluctantly matched Sam, and the hand was called: Sam slowly laid down three jacks, one at a time, giving each the whistle-and-boom sound of a falling bomb.

"As always, ladies, it's been a treat." Sam tugged his cap straight and scooped his haul into his knapsack while his friends griped. Jake threw himself onto his back like he had just died. "Hey now, winning four in a row is harder than it looks!" Sam assured them.

Sam closed his knapsack and stood up. The guys just sat there with grouchy faces. Mike was bored now and was throwing popcorn kernels at Jake's supine form. "Or maybe I was just born lucky. You wouldn't hold that against a guy, would ya?" Sam asked.

As Sam tugged his knapsack onto his back, something far beyond the fence caught his eye: someone on foot, alone and barely able to stand. No horse and no gun that he could see. The man tripped and went down. Sam flew down the ladder, running and calling after his sister, "Charlotte!"

2. Audience test your draft, and explain how this feedback can help you.

The audience test is online.

# Film

In the last eight chapters, you focused on the phase of filmmaking called development—you developed a script and film novel. In this chapter, you will start into the production phase. You will learn how to carry out the two main responsibilities of a director: creating a shooting script and storyboards, and auditioning and rehearsing actors. To learn the first responsibility, you will write a shooting script for a scene and video the scene with stand-ins. To learn the second, you will video the scene with actors. These activities will help you learn how to write for film directors and film actors. They will also help you know the qualities to look for in a director to film your novel. They may even set you on the path of directing your own film of your novel, as other film novelists have done.

### Week Fourteen

1. Read the introduction to this chapter and the assignments for weeks fourteen and fifteen. Write your questions; then read the chapter, and write your answers.
2. Pick a scene from a movie you like, and write a shooting script for it, with shot descriptions for each beat in the scene.
3. Pick a scene from your script, and write a shooting script for it, with shot descriptions for each beat in the scene. Use one shot or one pair of eye-matched shots per beat.
4. Create a video storyboard of your scene: video the scene with stand-in actors in an appropriate location, and then edit the shots together.
5. Audience test your video storyboard.

*Week Fifteen*

1. Pick an online scene with an actor you like in it, and write down the URL and the time code for the beat changes of the actor in the scene.
2. Audition and select actors for your scene. Video the audition, post it online, and indicate the time code for clips with the actors you want to use.
3. Have your actors memorize their lines, and rehearse the scene with them. Video the rehearsal and post it online.
4. Shoot the scene with the actors, and edit it together.
5. Audience test your video scene.

*Glossary*

| | |
|---|---|
| **blocking** | The positions and movements of actors and camera(s) |
| **point-of-view film** | A film with a point-of-view character or narrator for each scene |
| **shooting script** | A script that has shot descriptions for each beat of each scene |
| **storyboard** | A visualization of the shots in a shooting script, made with drawings, computer animation, or video |
| **video storyboard** | A video of the shots in a shooting script, made with stand-ins |
| **continuity shots** | Successive shots that look like shots of one continuous event |
| **jump cuts** | Discontinuous shots |
| **overlapping shots** | Successive shots that end and begin with the same action |

A director has numerous responsibilities, from analyzing a script with its plot and character development and theme, to assisting a producer in selecting a crew and cast, to endlessly consulting: What about this location? Will it help bring out the theme? What about this color scheme for costumes? Will it bring out the main turning points? What about this gesture, this lens for these shots, this sound effect for these scenes, this font for these titles? The questions go on and on, because it is the director's job to supervise a crew of filmmakers as they carry out their assigned responsibilities. But supervising the crew isn't the director's primary responsibility. The primary responsibility of the director is to block the scenes and work with actors.

## Blocking

Blocking is the placement of actors and camera(s) in a scene. It is called blocking because stage directors used to place blocks on a map of a stage to visually indicate the placement of actors. Good blocking brings out the beats in a scene visually. Bad blocking doesn't bring out the beats. Either it doesn't change the placement of actors and camera(s) when the beats change, or it changes their placement at other times, which happens often in films today.

To block a film scene, we first create what is called a *shooting script*. A shooting script indicates where the camera(s) should be placed in a scene, much like a film novel indicates (indirectly) where the reader is in a scene. In fact, once we have written a draft of a film novel and have, in the process, thought a lot about the placement of the reader in scenes, we are much better prepared to write a shooting script. The reverse is also true. Once we have written a shooting script and have, in the process, thought a lot about the placement of the camera in scenes, we are much better prepared to write a film novel. The two go hand in hand—starting with either one helps with the other.

## Shooting Script

To change a script into a shooting script, we first mark the beginning of each new beat in the script with a slash. Here is a simple example (which we will later add shot descriptions to):

```
INT. HOUSE—DAY

/John goes to the phone in the kitchen and stops,
his back to the camera.

/He picks up the phone, but it's dead.

/So he puts it down and leaves the room.

/He takes the phone by his nightstand, sits down
on the bed, and dials a number, but the line is
busy.

/He puts the phone down, watches it, and thinks
for a while.

/He tries again and gets through.

/He stands.
```

```
                    JOHN
        I have something to say.

                  MARTHA
        Okay.

    /He turns from the camera and braces himself
    against the wall.

                / JOHN
        I do want to marry you.
```

Now we add shot descriptions. There are two main types of shots that we describe—distance shots, which indicate how close the camera is to the subject(s); and framing shots, which indicate what is in the frame and where it is placed in the frame.

## Distance Shots

| | |
|---|---|
| **extreme wide shot (XWS)** | A shot that shows the subject(s) at a distance from the camera |
| **wide shot (WS)** | A shot that shows the complete subject(s) from head to toe |
| **medium shot (MS)** | A shot that shows the subject(s) from the waist up |
| **medium close up (MCU)** | A shot that shows the subject(s) from the arm-pits up |
| **close up (CU)** | A shot that shows a small part of the subject(s), like their face(s) from the top of their shoulders up |
| **extreme close up (XCU)** | A shot that shows a very small part of the subject(s), like their face(s) from above the chin to below the crown |

## Framing Shots

| | |
|---|---|
| **over the shoulder (OTS)** | A shot from over the shoulder of a subject, showing what the subject is looking at |
| **one shot (1S)** | A shot of one subject |
| **two shot (2S)** | A shot of two subjects |
| **reverse angle shots** | Shots of opposite sides of a subject, or in a dialogue scene, shots of each of the two participants |
| **eye-matching shots** | A pair of shots, one of a character looking at something and the other of what the character is looking at |

| | |
|---|---|
| **point-of-view shot (POV)** | In a pair of eye-matching shots, the shot of what a character is looking at |
| **tracking shot** | A shot that follows a subject by panning or moving the camera |
| **position tracking shot** | A tracking shot that keeps the subject in roughly the same position on screen, starting the movement when the subject is in that place on screen and stopping the movement when the subject is no longer in that place |
| **unmotivated move** | A movement of a camera that isn't tracking a subject—for example, one that is pushing in on a stationary subject |
| **establishing shot** | A shot showing a character and what the character is responding to |

In adding shot descriptions to a script, keep the following in mind: First, use establishing shots. Most film scenes start with an establishing shot of the main character in the scene—a shot wide enough to show where the character is and what the character is seeing or dealing with. But other film scenes delay establishing shots—for example, a director might start a scene with a close-up of a character coming into a room, cut to an eye-matched shot of the room, and then cut, as the character proceeds into the room, to an establishing shot. The early Russian filmmaker Pudovkin argued for a flexible use of establishing shots and illustrated how to use them creatively in his silent film *Mother*. As directors, we just need to remember to use establishing shots at appropriate points: start with one, or bring one in later, but bring one in at some appropriate point.

Second, follow the general practice of using closeups at the high points of scenes, when beats are intense. Close ups are often one shots, which means that close-up one shots often come at the high points of scenes. But there is another tradition of filmmaking that favors the use of close-up two shots at the high points, when characters are finally connecting well with each other in the scene. Jean Renoir once said that he thought characters in a love scene should be in two shots, not separate one shots.[1] A film that uses close-up two shots well is *The Kiss*, the last silent film of Marlene Dietrich. Renoir thought that the purpose of shooting in wide-screen format was to make close-up two shots possible, not to come up with something different to compete with television.[2] So remember, you can use close-up two shots when appropriate, not just close-up one shots.

Third, create continuity between the shots in a scene. Discontinuity occurs because films are usually shot with a camera that is shooting discontinuous events—the different "takes" of different "set ups"—but the shots, when put together in one scene, are supposed to be shots of one continuous event. The way to create continuity between successive shots is to make the shots different enough from each other that the viewer doesn't notice the small discontinuities that may occur from one shot to the next, like a character's hair being combed a little differently. There are several ways of creating continuity:

- Shoot a wide shot, then a close up (or vice versa)—for example, a wide shot of John at a table, then a close up of him.
- Shoot from one angle, then a different angle (at least 30 degrees different)—for example, a profile shot of John looking over the tables in a restaurant for Martha, then a frontal shot of him looking for her.
- Shoot a character starting a physical action, then finishing the action—for example, a shot of John starting to stand when Martha comes into view, then another shot of him as he finishes standing.
- Shoot a character from the front, then from the back (or vice-versa)—for example, a shot of John at the table from the front, then one of John from the back, perhaps from over his shoulder, showing what he sees.
- Shoot a character seeing something, then what the character is seeing (or vice-versa)—for example, a shot of John looking down at his menu, then a shot of the menu.
- Shoot a character completely leaving a shot, then entering the next shot (a clean exit); or a character starting to leave a shot, then completely entering the next shot (a clean entrance)—for example, a shot from outside the restaurant of Martha completely entering the restaurant, then a shot of her walking to the table.

Because audiences are so sensitive to changes in facial expressions, it is difficult, but not impossible, to cut with continuity between two shots of a person's face. When you want a face-to-face cut, use two or three of the first three techniques (which are the only ones applicable to face-to-face cuts): change distance, change angle, and/or cut on action (e.g., cut on an actor looking up).

Some films, like those for television, are shot with multiple cameras, so the continuity between shots is automatic—the cameras are shooting the same event. With multiple cameras, directors just need to be sure not to get one camera in the shot of another. Some directors use two cameras for conversations, because it is easy to set up the cameras out of each other's view. A good example of a conversation shot with two cameras is the one between the young couple in the restaurant in *Antoine Fisher* (the first film directed by Denzel Washington).

   If directors are shooting montage sequences, they may want discontinuity between the shots—so they may make what are called jump cuts. For example, a director might show a character in one shot shutting off his alarm and then in the next shot eating his breakfast. The gap in the action between these two shots would be big enough that it wouldn't look like a continuity mistake. In certain high points in scenes, some directors preserve audio continuity but not visual continuity. For example, throughout Susan Bier's film *Open Hearts*, continuous conversation takes place over increasingly discontinuous video. The first instance occurs when a woman initially talks to a doctor about the condition of her husband, who has been struck by a car.

   Fourth, indicate beat changes with a cut or a change in the movement of the camera, whichever results in the most natural movement of characters and camera. So if a cut requires unnatural movement of the actors to preserve continuity, indicate the beat change with a change in camera movement. For example, if a cut on a character in close up requires the character to awkwardly turn away from the camera just before the cut to preserve continuity, indicate the beat change with camera movement. On the other hand, if a change in the movement of the camera is too complex or too time consuming, then indicate the beat change with a cut. For example, if moving the camera from a distance to up close takes too long, then indicate the beat change with a cut. The most sensible approach, in deciding whether to cut or change camera movement at a beat change, is to choose the technique that allows the most natural movement of both the characters and the camera. That will result in scenes that have a natural mix of cutting and camera movement.

   Fifth, in each scene, establish a point-of-view character, or shoot the scene from the point of view of the narrator. There are several ways to establish a point-of-view character:

- Always show the main character or what that character is seeing or is about to see or has just seen.
- Track the main character and not others once the character is in the shot (unless the shot is a point-of-view shot of what that character is seeing).
- Shoot over the shoulder of the main character but not over the shoulders of the others in the scene.
- Shoot reverse-angle shots in a dialogue scene closer to the main character than to the other character in the scene.

**Figure 34  Antwone Fisher, 2002**

- Shoot a scene from the point of view of a voice-over narrator by changing the placement of characters and camera(s) when the beats of the
  voice-over change, much like music videos change visually when the
  phrases of music change.

Filmmaker Steven Katz writes, "Point of view, which may be the most
important aspect of a director's contribution, is handled indifferently in so
many films."[3] Only a few films handle point of view carefully.

A recent film that uses these basic point-of-view techniques beautifully is
Michael Haneke's *The White Ribbon* (a film often compared to Carl Dreyer's
films *Day of Wrath* and *Ordet*). Haneke starts the film with a voice-over
narrator and shoots every scene from the point of view of the voice-over
narrator or one of the characters, which makes the film feel like a novel.
He uses tracking shots, eye-matched shots, and over-the-shoulder shots to
establish the point-of-view character. He shoots the early, voice-over narrated scenes with an on-screen, point-of-view character, but as the film
develops, he shoots more of these narrated scenes from the point of view
of the narrator.

Haneke's favorite filmmaker, the Iranian director Abbas Kiarostami, also
shoots point-of-view films. Perhaps Kiarostami's most elaborate example is
the middle part of the film *Tickets* (the first and last parts were directed by
other filmmakers). In this film, he uses position tracking shots, eye-matched

**The White Ribbon, 2009**

Michael Haneke

shots, tight over-the-shoulder shots, and large close-ups of the point-of-view characters in reverse angle shots in dialogue scenes. He doesn't use a narrator. He often begins scenes with a medium position tracking shot, moves to an establishing two-shot, and then begins alternating one-shots. But what is perhaps most interesting is Kiarostami's increasing disruption of expected reverse-angle shots during dialogue scenes. After he moves in close on one character, he doesn't then move in close on the other, as we would expect. (Haneke also does this in a key scene in *Cache* at 50:07-53:51.) And increasingly toward the end of the film, he doesn't match a close up with *any* reverse angle shot. The effect is powerful. The technique is like the use of narrative asymmetries in the Bible. (In the Bible, reverse symmetries like AB C BA or forward symmetries like ABC ABC are highlighted by asymmetries in which expected matches don't occur—like AB C XA or ABC AB.[4] The Quran has similar symmetrical patterns with asymmetrical deviations. It may well be that behind Kiarostami's ground-breaking style (he didn't attend film school) are the rhetorical patterns of the Quran—patterns that Haneke has picked up on and brought to European films.

Three other Iranian point-of-view films are instructive to watch: *Offside,* by Jafar Panahi, Kiarostami's former assistant director, whose films were described by one critic as having a "tension between documentary

**Cache, 2005**

immediacy and a set of strictly defined formal parameters";[5] *The Smell of Camphor, Fragrance of Jasmine*, by USC-trained Bahman Farmanara, who first produced films by Kiarostami and who, in this film, builds to a climactic unmotivated camera move; and *Women's Prison*, the first feature film directed by Manijeh Hekmat, and perhaps the most moving of these three Iranian films.

Keeping these five ideas about shots in mind, let's return to the task of adding shot descriptions to our little scene about John. We number the shots and briefly describe them.

INT. HOUSE—DAY

*1. WS position tracking, then stopping*/John goes to the phone in the kitchen and stops, his back to the camera.

*2. CU*/He picks up the phone, but it's dead.

*3. MS on action, position tracking, clean exit*/So he puts it down and leaves the room.

*4. MS tracking*/He takes the phone by his night-stand, sits down on the bed, and dials a number, but the line is busy.

*5a. CU on phone, alternating with eye-match, 6. CU of John*/He puts the phone down, watches it, and thinks for a while.

*5b. CU of phone, tracking to John's ear/*He tries again and gets through.

*7a. MS on action/*He stands.

> JOHN
>
> I have something to say.

> MARTHA
>
> Okay.

*7b. MS reframing John/*He turns from the camera and braces himself against the wall.

*8. CU/*          JOHN
          I do want to marry you.

Notice that each beat has just one shot or a pair of eye-matched shots (shots 5 and 6). Notice, also, that two shots cover more than one beat (shots 5 and 7). But in both cases, the camera changes from being stationary to tracking, indicating beat changes.

## Video Storyboards

A shooting script gives us a list of shots we need to shoot. What it doesn't give us is an idea of how to frame these shots. For that we need storyboards. Storyboards are pictures of the shots in a scene. Storyboards can be drawn—for example, using stick figures—or they can be built with fancy computer animation programs like MovieStorm. But the simplest ones are video storyboards. Here is how you make them:

First, find a location for your scene (or maybe a location that simulates the location you eventually want to use).

Second, stage the scene at the location. Show some stand-ins how and where to move in the scene and when to read their lines. Tell them to make definite starting and stopping movements, not indefinite ones, and to drop or adjust any changes in movements that don't coincide with the beats in the scene.

Third, frame each shot so that it has a focal point and is balanced. A focal point is something that catches our attention—our eyes hover around it, going to it first and frequently returning to it. The focal point of a shot should be the main character in the scene or what that character is looking at. Here is how to make one:

- Put it close to the camera, so it is large on screen.
- Shoot it from the front, not the side.

- Put it to the left of the screen (people who read from left to right look to the left first).
- Place it where lines of things lead to it.
- Frame it by putting something around it, like a window or a doorway.
- Give it a color or brightness that contrasts with what is around it.

A shot is balanced when it doesn't seem like it wants to tip over. As you create balance, consider these points:

- Balance can be symmetrical, with things of equal weight at equal distances from the middle line—like two equal-sized children on a teeter-totter at equal distances from the fulcrum.
- Balance can be asymmetrical, with things of greater weight closer to the middle line—like two unequal-sized children on a teeter-totter, the bigger child closer to the fulcrum.
- A profile shot of a character looking at something creates weight in the direction of the look. So to balance a profile shot of a character looking at something, don't put the character in the middle of the shot—put the character to the side opposite the direction of the look.

Fourth, video each shot in the shooting script, using an inexpensive video camera. For each shot, shoot more of the scene than you intend to use. Start each shot early and end it late, so that the ending of each shot overlaps the beginning of the next shot. For example, assume you are shooting a medium shot of a character starting to stand up and then cutting to a close up of the character finishing the stand. If you begin the shots early and end them late, the end of the medium shot will overlap the beginning of the close up, and you can cut between the two shots somewhere in the middle of the stand. Also, if your shot descriptions for a scene call for the same shot in two non-sequential beats, video the two shots at the same time. For example, if you have the same shot description for a beginning and an ending establishing shot in a scene, shoot both of the shots, one right after the other, from one camera setup. Then you won't have to set up the same shot twice. To make the process easier for the actors, you may want to simply set up the first shot and shoot the whole scene from that position and then later cut out the in-between part and replace it with close-up shots.

Finally, edit the shots together with a simple software program like MovieMaker or iMovies. Cut right on a beat change if that feels appropriate. Or cut slightly before the beat change when you can sense that the beat is soon coming to an end. Or cut slightly after the beat change when you can sense the new beat has started.

## Audience Test

Once you have created a video storyboard of your scene, audience test it. Show it to friends and ask them (1) if they think they understand what the main character is doing, and (2) if they think the way the video was shot helps them to understand what the character is doing. Once you have a positive audience test, go on to find actors for the scene.

## Directing Actors

The second major responsibility of directors is to audition and rehearse actors. The key, in both auditioning and rehearsing, is to realize that reflection and practice provide resources for actors to draw from during performance. In the words of the great Russian acting theorist Stanislavski, we "combine [our memories] in one way or another" during performance.[6] In terms of process philosophy, thought and practice provide potentialities for actors to creatively actualize in performance. Some pianists practice music loudly and slowly, so that their hand movements get into their muscle memory. Then they can draw on that memory

**Constantin Stanislavski**

in performance. Some wrestlers practice moves slowly, so that they can physically remember those moves in the press of the moment. Basketball players imagine their moves. Reflection and practice create memories, and these memories are potentialities that performers draw from in the moment of creation.

Here is a simple plan for auditioning and rehearsing actors. It is grounded in the fundamentals of Stanislavski's theories and can be easily carried out before and during an actual shoot. Carrying out such a plan with all the actors will prevent the uneven quality of acting so common in independent films, which often have only a few seasoned actors.

## Auditioning Actors

Ask your actors to come with specific lines from the script memorized. You want to see how well they can perform when their lines are memorized.

During the audition, ask your actors to carry out some physical actions—for example, to walk here and pick up this, sit there and turn that way, etc.—while they deliver their lines and your assistants read the lines of the other characters in the scene. Let your actors practice the movements a few times, and see if they can deliver their lines without focusing on the movements they are supposed to be carrying out. See if they can respond in the moment to the lines your assistants are reading.

Also, ask your actors to interpret what their characters are doing. Ask them to interpret their characters' actions in ways that make those actions seem reasonable. Actors must believe that the actions of their characters are reasonable or they won't be able to perform them convincingly.

Everyone has his reasons, says one of Renoir's characters in *The Rules of the Game*. Even evil characters have their reasons. The Joker, in *The Dark Knight*, for example, believes he is helping people realize that they can't control their lives. He doesn't believe he is trying to wreak havoc on Gotham City. He is obsessed with the good he is doing, not the evil.

**Rules of the Game, 1939**

Once your actors have interpreted their characters' actions in a way that makes them seem reasonable, ask them to deliver their lines again, without thinking about their interpretations.

Then pick some promising actors, and try them in pairs. Ask them to explain to each other what their characters are doing. Then ask them to deliver their lines, again without thinking about their interpretations. See if they can connect to each other, listen to each other, and draw from the potentialities of each other's performance in the moment.

Once you have chosen actors, ask them to memorize all their lines before the shoot. Tell them to practice saying their lines aloud, quickly and flatly—to memorize words, not intonations, which will come in the moment of performance.

## Rehearsing Actors

At the shoot, have your actors walk through the blocking for their scene. Make any needed adjustments to their blocking.

Then, while your cameramen practice shots and set lights, have the actors practice their lines together, saying them quickly and flatly, to make sure they have the words memorized.

Then discuss the scene with your actors. It is important to involve all the actors, Stanislavski believed,[7] because actors need to interpret all of the characters in their scene well so they won't dismiss each other's views as ridiculous. As you discuss the scene, (1) tell your actors what has happened in the scenes just before the scene they will be performing. (2) Ask them to sympathetically summarize their main action in the scene. (Have them do so simply and succinctly, so they won't have to think about their interpretations during performance. An actor, for example, should say he is trying to calm someone, not that he is once again trying to motivate this person who has been cheated to respond calmly even when provoked to anger.) (3) Then have them summarize the beats in their scene, including whether the actions in their beats are to be done quickly or slowly. (They may want to divide the scene into more beats than you did for the shots, and their way of summarizing the beats may be different than yours, but these variations may still be appropriate for the scene.) (4) Ask them what new thoughts or feelings or intentions their characters have come to by the end of the scene. (5) Finally, ask them to describe the thoughts and images (subtext) that might go through their heads during the scene. Encourage them to come up with what they personally believe would be most reasonable for

**The Dark Knight, 2008**

someone in that situation to think and imagine. Your job, as Jean Renoir said, is to bring out "the personality of the actor within the framework of a defined role.".[8]

Then have your actors practice any movements or gestures or intonations that may be useful but difficult to carry out in the scene.

Also, have your actors practice listening to each other, communing in the moment, as Stanislavski puts it,[9] by talking together and repeating each other's last line, only changing personal pronouns, as in the following:

A: How are you?
B: How am I? Fine, I guess. I have felt better before.
A: You have felt better before. What's wrong? Tell me.
B: Tell you. Okay, if you're ready.

Ask them to empathetically reflect each other's tone as they begin speaking but to give the other actor a different tone to pick up on as they finish speaking. Ask them to do this without thinking about doing it. Once everything is close to being ready for them on set, ask your actors to begin to get into character by focusing on what their characters would be focusing on.

At this point, your actors should be retreating and their characters stepping forward.

## On Set

On set ask your actors to focus their attention on what is happening in the scene moment by moment. If you notice them instead focusing on what they are supposed to be doing, ask them to "forget" their preparation and just do what comes to them in the moment as they hear each other's lines and see each other's actions. (Of course, they won't fully forget their preparation. It will peripherally affect them as they draw from its potentialities in the moment.) [10]

To help them respond in the moment, you may need to ask them to notice something in the scene that they haven't noticed before—a detail about the set or a costume or a gesture of another actor. If they keep forgetting something they need to do—like where to move—take time out and practice what they need to do a few times. Then have them return to responding in the moment.

Then have your actors rehearse the scene in front of the camera until they are performing distinct beats within an overall integrated action for the scene. That combination—diversity of beats in a unified scene—is what you find the best actors creating—actors like Jack Nicholson, Anthony Hopkins, and Meryl Streep.

We have worked with actors in feature films this way, asking them to summarize and practice their scenes, then forget their summaries and practice and simply focus on responding to what is happening in the moment. We have been pleased with both the process and the results.

## Audience Test

After you have created your scene with actors, audience test it. Show it to your friends and ask them (1) if they think they understand what the main character is doing, and (2) if they think the acting helps them understand what the character is doing.

## Student Writing Group

### Week Fourteen

1. Read the introduction to this chapter and the assignments for weeks fourteen and fifteen. Write your questions; then read the chapter, and write your answers.

*Do we really need to video our scene twice—once with stand-ins for the storyboards and once with actors?* Videoing the storyboard is a preliminary step. We cheaply and quickly film the scene and audience test it before investing more time and energy in doing the real thing.

2. Pick a scene from a movie you like and write a shooting script for it, with shot descriptions for each beat in the scene.

Our shooting script for our movie scene is online.

3. Pick a scene from your script, and write a shooting script for it, with shot descriptions for each beat in the scene. Use one shot or one pair of eye-matched shots per beat.

```
EXT. LIBERTY COMMUNITY FORT LOOKOUT—MORNING

1. XWS BIRDSEYE / Bustle of community alongside
the fort boardwalk. We hear four boys chatting.

2a. WS on the boys/ Four boys sit on the boards
playing poker, munching: SAM, seated leftmost in
frame, wears his "lucky cap;" clockwise from him are
MIKE, JAKE, and NATHAN. Sam picks up the deck.

3. CU on Sam's work-toughened but youthful hands/
He is expertly shuffling a deck of cards against
the wood floor. His hand shoos a few tiny white but-
terflies away.

4a. MS on Sam, 5a. WS on THREE BOYS/ He enjoys
entertaining his friends.

                    SAM
           Watch this!

Mike, at Sam's left, and Nathan, at right, are
impressed. Jake eats his sandwich and looks at
Sam's face.

4b. MS on Sam, 6a. MS on Jake/ Sam notices Jake is
looking at his face, not watching the show. Sam
frowns. Jake, grinning as he eats, stares at Sam.

                    SAM (CONT'D)
         ·  What?

Jake giggles, coughs on an inhaled crumb. He holds
up a finger to indicate wait.
```

*4c. MS on Sam, 7a. MS on Nathan/* Sam stops shuffling
and cocks his chin at Nathan.

                    SAM (CONT'D)
          Hit me!

Nathan smiles and lobs a chocolate high. Sam moves
into place and catches it in his mouth. Nathan
fist-pumps, eats a chocolate, and tosses the foil
wrapper.

                    NATHAN
          That's three for three!

*5b. WS on Jake and Mike and Nathan/* Jake keeps
laughing as he tries to talk.

                    JAKE
          Sam, my brother wants me
          to ask you … um … Jason
          wants to know if you think
          Charlotte likes him!

Mike and Nathan howl with laughter and dig into
caramel popcorn. Sitting between them, Jake
reacts.

*4d. MS on Sam, 6b. MS on Jake/* Sam continues to
shuffle.

                    SAM
               (deadpan, to Jake)
          Jason? Sorry. Not interested.

                    JAKE
          At least ask her! You don't know
          what she'll say.

*2b. WS on THE BOYS/* Jake pulls the popcorn away
from Mike, who snatches it back. Sam is absentmindedly listening as he shuffles.

                    MIKE (O.S.)
          C'mon, Sam! Just deal!

*4e. MS on Sam 5c. WS on the THREE BOYS/*

```
                    SAM
              (to Jake)
        But  I  DO  know  Jason—and
        Brock,  and  Kevin,  and  the
        guy with the goats … ?

                  NATHAN
        Elliott?

                    SAM
              (points at Nathan, nods)
        Elliott.
```

Jake is growing discouraged.

*8. CU on Sam, 9. CU on Jake/*

```
                  SAM (CONT'D)
        Gentlemen,  I  am  the first  line
        of defense.
```

*2c. WS on BOYS/* Sam begins to deal the hand.

```
                  SAM (CONT'D)
        No smelly guy is dating my sister
        without my approval.
```

Mike sniffs his armpit. Jake sighs and watches Sam deal.

4. Create a video storyboard of your scene: video the scene with stand-in actors in an appropriate location, and then edit the shots together.

   Our video storyboard is online.

5. Audience test your video storyboard.

   Our audience test is online.

## Week Fifteen

1. Pick an online scene with an actor you like in it, and write down the URL and the time code for the beat changes of the actor in the scene.

   Our scene with an actor we like is posted online.

2. Audition and select actors for your scene. Video the audition, post it online, and indicate the time code for clips with the actors you want to use.

Our audition is posted online.

3. Have your actors memorize their lines, and rehearse the scene with them. Video the rehearsal and post it online.

   Our rehearsal is posted online.

4. Shoot the scene with the actors, and edit it together.

   Our scene is posted online.

5. Audience test your video scene.

   Our audience test is online.

# Conclusion

Film novels are short novels that have enough description to keep readers picturing scenes. These novels are well written when they continually engage readers in generously interpreting the story, the characters, and the narrator. Film novels are still in their youth as a literary form, but they have come from a rich tradition of descriptive fiction, a tradition well underway before the advent of films. They have yet to fully realize their potential.

Many film novels are simple, with only dialogue and description. But film novels can be more complex. They can use flashbacks, flash-forwards, and imaginings. They can use narration throughout montage sequences of short scenes and at the beginnings and endings of long scenes, as in films like *The Magnificent Ambersons*, *My Dog Skip*, and *Blow*. Or they can use narration on and off throughout scenes, as in *The Thin Red Line,* whose characters periodically speak in voice-over; *Diary of a Country Priest*, whose narrator speaks the words we often see him writing in his diary; and *My Father's Glory*, which depicts scenes from the childhood of the narrator, who intermittently talks about his family.

Film novels and the films based on them can have strong lines of action, which support strong character development, which supports strong themes. They can have strong stylistic elements that bring out their themes—like

**The Magnificent Ambersons, 1942**

the beat-by-beat development of point-of-view characters and narrators. As a result, they can call audiences to synthesize their past understanding of themselves and the world with their emerging understanding of what they are reading and seeing. I have written this book in hopes of seeing film novels and films based on them flourish in these ways.

## Student Writing Group

This is Madeleine again, your up-and-coming film novelist, who, in doing these assignments with the help of my good friend Mel, has written more versions of *Against a Crooked Sky* than your readers may have wanted to read. Now that we've traversed reams of paper together, burned barrels of midnight oil, and likely eaten more chocolate than I'll ever admit, I have a couple of closing thoughts on this whole hairy journey. In my introduction to the student writing group, I both lamented and welcomed the challenge that lay before me with the pithy statement, "When the way is hard, the end is beautiful." (By the way, Dr. Packard, I'm still going to check the citations to make sure you've included me as a professional quotist.) But I have to recant that statement because I've discovered that it is incomplete. What? Fine. I won't *recant* it—I'll just *complete* it: "When the way is hard, *but you trust the process and stick with it*, the end can be beautiful." I won't lie and say there weren't moments when I was pulling my hair out. I looked into buying stock in Rogaine. And Tums. And midnight oil. But as I trudged along, those moments when the fabulous filmic light bulb came on for me were just frequent enough to keep me intrigued and invested in finding out where this ride would take me. Let's just say I recently commissioned a small marble sculpture of a light bulb for my mantle.

So tell those people (other budding film novelists like me) for whom the process might sometimes feel like trying to build a Lego skyscraper while some brainiac little kid keeps telling you you're doing it wrong—"*No, no-*

**My Father's Glory, 1990**

*you skipped the lateral support widget, and you have no flux capicitrons!*"—tell them not to be surprised when they step back and realize they haven't built a skyscraper: they've built a *rocket*. And tell them, while they're out buying paper by the ream, they might pick up a barrel of midnight oil and a case or two of chocolate. Rocket fuel comes from unlikely places.

# Appendix
# Suggested Readings

## Short Stories

"Hills Like White Elephants," by Ernest Hemingway
"The Girls in Their Summer Dresses," by Irwin Shaw
"The Petrified Man," by Eudora Welty
"Snow," by Charles Baxter
"The Heavenly Animal," by Jayne Anne Phillips
"Say Yes," by Tobias Wolff

## Novels

*The Duel,* by Anton Chekhov
*The Maltese Falcon,* by Dashiell Hammett
*Sanctuary,* by William Faulkner
*In Dubious Battle,* by John Steinbeck
*Of Mice and Men,* by John Steinbeck
*The Chips Are Down,* by Jean-Paul Sartre
*The Misfits,* by Arthur Miller
*Loving,* by Henry Green
*Losing Battles,* by Eudora Welty

## Screenplays

www.script-o-rama.com

# The Possibility of Film Novels

The burgeoning study of the relationship between novels and films, increasingly a major part of university curricula, has revolved around film novels. This can be seen in the writings of four major theorists: George Bluestone, Edward Murry, Bruce Morrissette, and Timothy Corrigan. Their writings address two major questions about film novels: what are they, and can they be well written and well filmed?

George Bluestone's *Novels into Film* (1957) was the first book-length treatment of the relationship between novels and films. The overall project of his book is to answer this question: What can be transferred to film? As Bluestone explains, when people complain that a novel hasn't been faithfully adapted to film, they often assume that the whole novel could have been transferred to film.[1] They not only ignore what Bluestone calls "the governing conventions" of the two media, namely, "their different audiences, different modes of production, and different censorship requirements,"[2] but they also ignore the fact that some things may be impossible to transfer to film.[3] Bluestone writes, "Like two intersecting lines, novel and film meet at a point, then diverge." At the point of divergence are what he calls scenario-novels: "At the intersection, the book and shooting script are almost indistinguishable. But where the lines diverge, they not only resist conversion; they also lose all resemblance to each other."[4] Scenario-novels are the touchstone, then, for what can be transferred to film. Only with a scenario-novel can we ask why a novel wasn't faithfully adapted and do so knowing it could have all been transferred to film—the "governing conventions" allowing.

But what exactly do these scenario-novels consist of? Since Bluestone says that scenario-novels are almost indistinguishable from movie scripts, we can find his answer to this question by looking at what he calls "the essential ingredients of a movie script." Bluestone writes that the novel *Pride and Prejudice* possesses these "essential ingredients."[5] The first ingredient he mentions is "a lack of particularity." By that he means the "absence of minute physical detail."[6] He says that Jane Austen's characters and things are "never rendered with the exact brush strokes of the painter." But he observes that the author's "sparse detail in no way diminishes the imaginative force of the characterization"; instead, the details give us a "thorough psychological

**Jane Austen**

delineation" of the characters.[7] Two other "essential ingredients of a movie script," he claims, are "an absence of metaphorical language" and an "insistence on absolute clarity,"[8] which he also calls a "clean" style.[9] "Jane Austen's novel further resembles a shooting-script," Bluestone continues, "in that its point of view is omniscient."[10] By that he means the author shifts from one point-of-view character to another, which film often does: "Traditionally, the camera has resembled the narrative mind in Tolstoy, say, where we move from one point of view to another, rather than Lambert Strether's unitary vision in *The Ambassadors*," which is always from one character's point of view.[11] "Finally, [*Pride and Prejudice*] resembles the scenario in its heavy reliance on dialogue to advance plot and reveal character."[12]

In short, Bluestone is saying that the "essential ingredients" of a scenario-novel are describing only details relevant to characterization, using a clean and nonmetaphorical style, using multiple point-of-view characters and relying heavily on dialogue. But are these ingredients essential? Suppose a novelist were to (1) describe the walls of a room as light blue when that fact wasn't relevant to characterization, or (2) metaphorically describe a group of students in a library as bathed in a dreary atmosphere, or (3) use just one point-of-view character, or (4) use a lot of interior monologue in scenes. Any one of these could still be transferred to a script. Bluestone's "essential ingredients" may correctly characterize Jane Austen's novel, and they may make a scenario-novel a better novel, but they don't seem to be necessary to make a novel transferrable to a film script and so can't be considered essential ingredients of a scenario-novel itself.

In his last chapter, Bluestone adds another "essential ingredient" of scenario-novels: "While novels may be divided into those which resemble the movie scenario and those which do not, we find, increasingly, scenario-novels being taken over by the cinema, interior-subjective novels refusing such transfer."[13] Scenario-novels, he is saying, aren't interior-subjective

**Forrest Gump, 1994**

novels. Presumably this means they don't include interior-subjective elements like interior monologues, subjective narration, memories, dreams, and imagination, which Bluestone claims aren't handled well by films.[14] But filmscripts can certainly include interior monologues (e.g., *About a Boy*), subjective narration (*Shawshank Redemption*), memories (*Forrest Gump*), dreams (*Antwone Fisher*), and imagination (*Better Off Dead*), so scenario-novels could include them as well.

Bluestone's idea that film novels rely on dialogue is reiterated by the writer Edward Murray. In his book *The Cinematic Imagination: Writers and the Motion Pictures* (1972), Murray writes about "movie novels."[15] In his observations about two of Steinbeck's novels, we find what he considers to be the characteristics of movie novels: "Everything in *In Dubious Battle* is presented in action and dialogue; the author scrupulously avoids internal revelation of character," and *The Red Pony* "is told almost entirely in description and dialogue."[16] Murray contrasts the ingredients of these novels with the narrative summary Steinbeck uses in earlier novels.[17] Generalizing Murray's characterization of *In Dubious Battle* and *The Red Pony*, we can say that, for Murray, movie novels consist entirely of dialogue and description of scenes. But, again, because film scripts can include more than just dialogue and description of scenes (e.g., voice-over narration), movie novels can as well.

In his book *Novel and Film: Essays in Two Genres* (1985),[18] Bruce Morrissette articulates a more current perspective on film novels. He explains the role that "contemporary cinema novels (which the French call *ciné-romans*)" can play in the discovery of what he calls a "unified field" between films and novels[19]—that is, a common source from which films and novels emerge. Cinema novels are a "rather limited group of works," Morrissette explains, but they constitute "a microcosm of the wider area of cinema and novel in general" that sheds "light on a 'unified field' approach to the fictional structures and perspectives to be found in both novel and film."[20] In other words, the "coexistence and parallelism of film/novel structures," which corresponds to the "field of the cinema novel,"[21] suggests the existence of a unified field between films and novels.

What could a unifying field between films and novels be? As Morrisette explains, a unifying field could be a field of analogous "fictional structures,"[22] jointly evolving,[23] reciprocally influencing each other, or converging due to shared influences.[24] Or it could be a unifying psychological field: that is, there could exist "beyond the words on the page and beyond the images on the screen as well, a common field of the imagination in which the work of art—visual, auditory, or verbal—takes on its effective aesthetic form and meaning."[25] In other words, it could be that "film and novel, so different in their material aspects, in their psychological dynamics, in their technical modes (and yet so comparable), come together" in a type of "inner screen of the brain" to form a "unified field of inner aesthetic response."[26] Or, as he only hints at, there may be, not merely a common psychological field, but a common physiological one.[27] That is, physiological responses may underlie the perception of both images and words. Finally, the unifying field could be a matter of shared ends. For example, an "aim of the film," like that of the novel, could be "the artistic creation of psychological or aesthetic effects."[28]

The discovery of a unified field, Morrissette writes, wouldn't imply that films and novels are the same genre,[29] but that there are equivalencies between them. As he explains, "all the theoretical objections that have been plausibly raised against equivalency" have not put a stop to searching for and finding parallel or analogous methods in novels and films.[30] Time and again, it is tempting, he writes, when watching "some new effect in the movies" to say "the novel could never do *that*" or vice-versa.[31] But, as he illustrates with dissolves and nonsynchronous sounds and images, filmmakers and novelists keep finding analogous ways of doing things.[32]

Finding a unified field between films and novels, Morrissette explains, would help us understand "two associated phenomena: a progressive internationalization and at the same time a more and more widespread mixing or melding of art forms, from the literary to the visual, the auditory, the filmic." That is, a unified field would help explain why artistic creations are taking on similar forms in nearly all countries and in almost all spheres of artistic creativity.[33]

The cinema novel, Morrissette claims, evolved as a type of film script. Initially, films were made from already written sources, such as plays, novels, or stories: "The early period of the silent film was marked by the priority of written sources for scenarios."[34] Then scenarios "structured like the novels that had already influenced the cinema" began to be written for films:[35]

> Some of these scenarios were published. They were silent film scripts with a few subtitles [in addition to description] but without dialogues, as, for example, the text of *Un Chien Andalou* by Dali and Buñuel. This scenario is a good example of the earliest attempts to use verbal descriptions to suggest to a reader the visual images of the screen. Had the sound film not come into existence at about this time, no doubt a considerable development of silent film scripts would have occurred.[36]

"Eventually," he continues, "with the contemporary cinema novel, the novelized script made its appearance."[37] He cites as an example, Jean-Paul Sartre's *Les Jeux sont faits* (*The Chips Are Down*) (1947), which he calls "one of the earliest works that may be called a true cinema novel, the deliberate creation of an author who composed his text originally to be filmed."[38]

A cinema novel, Morrissette explains, consists, like a script, of a mixture of "sound and image ... in written form."[39] He includes as sounds everything in a film "from realistic conversational exchanges to commentary, soliloquy, voiced memory, and the like."[40] He doesn't count as cinema novels those novels in which actual "visual images seen on the screen" are put on the edge of each page adjacent to the text: "The result no longer gives the impression of a real cinema novel and instead appears as an illustrated text, in the style of the Italian 'photo novels.'"[41] For a "model of the cinema novel," Morrissette puts forward the printed form of *Marienbad* by Alain Robbe-Grillet, who took a script "complete in every detail of dialogue and visual images," and simply reformatted it for "the printed cinema novel."[42] In short, for Morrissette, cinema novels are sounds and images for films, formatted like novels. His definition, as long as we understand sounds to include interior monologue and voice over, may be accurate, but it isn't cast in the literary terms that writers could readily apply to their art.

Timothy Corrigan, in his book *Film and Literature: An Introduction and Reader* (1999), traces the prehistory and history of the relationships between film and literature from the late eighteenth century through the twentieth century, and includes a discussion of film novels. He explains that recent discussions about relationships between film and literature "[seem] more lively than ever before, both inside and outside the classroom." This is due in part to "the cultural questioning of artistic hierarchies and canons" and

**David Griffith**

in part to "the increased mixing of different media in both literary and film practices." The result, in universities, is that "isolated media and literature departments now share materials, students and methods." He writes, "We increasingly admit and take seriously many different exchanges between literary works and films. Novels, dramatic literature, short stories, poetry, and even the essay have particular counterparts in film form."[43]

Corrigan gives historical examples of how film and literature have influenced each other, from the silent era to the present: filmmaker D. W. Griffith, at the turn of the century, borrowed techniques of "visual and temporal movement" from Dickens.[44] American novelists of the 1930s "[recast] in language ... film's panoramic visual movements, its fragmentary montages of images [and] its documentary clarity."[45] The film noir movies of the 1940s imitated the "multiple plot lines and narrative gaps in the action" of popular detective fiction.[46] In a number of literary and art film collaborations during the 1950s and 1960s, writers and filmmakers shared not only "subject matter" but "structural organizations."[47] During the late 1960s and through the 1970s, a number of novels and their film versions were published and produced simultaneously.[48] In the 1980s and 1990s, multimedia companies commissioned novelizations of film scripts to be released with films.[49]

In a chapter entitled "Books and Movies as Multimedia: Into the 1990s," Corrigan explains that "many popular novels today appear aimed at film adaptation even when they are first published as novels," and "their style and structure could be considered already that of a novelization [a novel made from a script]."[50] He states that the most film-like of these novels are what the French call "cinema novels" and others call "film novels" or "movie novels."[51] These novels, he explains, use "language and formal shapes" that "mimic or approach the forms and structures used by the cinema."[52] In other words, their "imagistic textuality approaches cinematic forms."[53] Corrigan doesn't get more specific than this.

From Bluestone and Murray to Morrissette and Corrigan, the discussion about novel/film relationships has centered around film novels. But the discussants haven't defined them much better than Carl Dreyer did eighty years ago when he called them film scripts in the form of novels—a definition that uses film terms to characterize them. As Morrissette points out, "Forms not previously recognized" in one domain can be recognized with the help of terms from another domain.[54] But, he continues, after the forms are identified, terms from the original domain can be used to define them.[55] In literary terms, film novels could be defined like this: novels of about 30,000 words of scene description interspersed in dialogue or interior monologue or narration.

The second question addressed by these four theorists of novel/film relationships is this: Can film novels be well written and well filmed? Early scholars, concerned about preserving the differences between film and novels, were skeptical about the possibility of film novels being written and filmed well. Bluestone concludes that though scenario novels can be transferred to film, "the film and the novel remain separate institutions, each achieving its best results by exploring unique and specific properties."[56] But Bluestone doesn't argue his case convincingly. To show that the best results are obtained by exploring unique and specific properties of novels and films, he would have to show that scenario-novels don't make for both the best novels and the best films. That he doesn't show. But Murray attempts to show it.

Murray's view of movie novels is evident in a passage from the last few pages of his book *The Cinematic Imagination*: "Of late, book reviewers and

**Virginia Woolf**

literary critics have become skillful at identifying the 'movie novel.' The species can be known by its skin-deep characterizations, its structure of truncated scenes, its jump-cut transitions, its dialogue intended to complement the screen image, and its theme which can be projected in one picture without a thousand words."[57] His negative characterization of movie novels echoes an earlier author he quotes at some length—Virginia Woolf.

Murray cites an article by Woolf called "The 'Movie' Novel," which appeared in the *Times Literary Supplement* in 1918. In the article, she attacks a novel she calls a movie novel—Compton Mackenzie's *The Early Life and Adventures of Sylvia Scarlett*.[58] She writes that its shallow characters don't measure up to memorable ones in past novels, like Moll Flanders and Tom Jones:

Compared with Mr. Mackenzie's characters [Moll Flanders and Tom Jones] are a slow-moving race... But consider how many things we know about them ... without a word of description perhaps, but merely because they are themselves. We can think about them when we are no longer reading the book. But we cannot do this with Mr. Mackenzie's characters; and the reason is, we fancy, that though Mr. Mackenzie can see them once he can never see them twice, and, as in a cinema, one picture must follow another without stopping, for if it stopped and we had to look at it we should be bored. Now, it is a strange thing that no one has yet been seen to leave a cinema in tears. The cab horse bolts down Haverstock-hill and we think it a good joke; the cyclist runs over a hen, knocks an old woman into the gutter, and has a hose turned upon him. But we never care whether he is wet or hurt or dead. So it is with Sylvia Scarlett and her troupe. Up they get and off they go, and as for minding what becomes of them, all we hope is that they will, if possible, do something funnier next time. No, it is not a book of adventures; it is a book of cinema.[59]

Woolf is saying, then, that we don't know anything about the characters in "movie novels" except what they are described as doing, so that if we were to stop reading for a moment, we would have nothing to think about. In short, the description conveys nothing about the characters except their behavior. But surely that characteristic needn't be true of movie novels in general. The thoughts and feelings of characters could be suggested by descriptions of their gestures and by their dialogue. (Of course, dialogue in the silent movies of 1918 played a much smaller role in revealing character than it does today.)

Murray makes two claims: (1) Movie novels—that is, script-like novels that don't include interior-subjective elements—are too technically restricted to make good novels, even if they now and then make good films. Movie novels, he says, are "scenarios[s] pretending to be fiction."[60] (2) Script-like novels that do include interior-subjective elements, like long stretches of Joyce and Faulkner, don't make good films.[61] Given those two assumptions, the conclusion follows that script-like novels don't make for both good novels and good films. Hence, we can draw Bluestone's conclusion that films and novels are "separate institutions, each achieving its best results by exploring unique and specific properties." The question is whether Murray has adequately supported his two assumptions.

Murray assumes, but doesn't argue, that novels of dialogue and description can't be successful novels, even though many novels have successful scenes of just dialogue and description, and some successful short stories are just dialogue and description, like Hemingway's *Hills Like White Elephants*.

It thus isn't obvious that short novels of dialogue and description can't be successful.

Nor does Murray make a convincing case for the other prong of his argument, which is that script-like novels with interior-subjective elements, though they may be successful novels, won't make successful films. He offers some evidence that such successful script-like novels haven't been made into successful films, but he doesn't show that they *couldn't* be made into successful films. When Murray discusses the idea of transferring James Joyces's *Ulysses* to film, he recognizes that long stretches of *Ulysses* are script-like, with interior-subjective elements that could be transferred to film as interior monologue, subjective narration, memories, dreams, and imagination. In fact, Murray writes, "It is no exaggeration to say that *Ulysses* contains equivalents for almost every conceivable filmic technique."[62] In Joseph Strick's film adaptation of *Ulysses* (1967), we find a full range of film techniques used to convey the interior-subjective elements of the novel. But Murray believes that "viewers unfamiliar with the novel would not understand the screen version and hence would be bored by the proceedings."[63] He is convinced that no filmmaker, no matter how talented, could do justice to *Ulysses*, given "the inherent limitations of the medium" of film.[64]

But, even if it were true that novels as complex as *Ulysses* couldn't be understood at the speed film unfolds, that doesn't mean that simpler, but still successful script-like novels with interior-subjective elements couldn't be successfully filmed. Murray ignores the large number of films that have used interior-subjective elements. Many of these films are critically

**It's a Wonderful Life, 1946**

acclaimed, like *Citizen Kane*, or popular ones, like *It's a Wonderful Life*. It isn't obvious that successful script-like novels couldn't have been written for such films. It may well be true that trying to preserve the interior-subjective elements of most novels would result in disastrous films. But that fact doesn't show that a film novel with interior-subjective elements couldn't make a successful film.

Murray, then, hasn't adequately argued that films and novels are separate art forms with unique qualities that make them good or successful. Murray worries that more and more "dramatists are presenting film scenarios in the guise of plays,"[65] and that novelists are so confounding fiction and film that, under the guise of writing novels, they are really turning out scenarios.[66] He worries that "eventually, a complete confusion of art forms may come about as novels become nearly totally cinematic and films become increasingly novelized."[67] That would be terrible only if it could be shown, as Murray hasn't, that script-like novels can't make for both successful novels and successful films.[68]

Later scholars, more concerned about similarities between film and novels, are much more optimistic about the prospects of film novels being well written and well filmed. For Morrissette, film novels are an alternative to "blindly taking refuge in out-of-date dogmas of sealed off, inviolable genres" and turning our "back[s] on the most innovative and exciting forms of our times."[69] The recent acceptance of deep similarities between film and novels, seen for example in Morrissette and Corrigan, finds expression in the words of novelist Graham Greene—many of whose novels were adapted to film: "There is no need to regard the cinema as a completely new art; in its fictional form it has the same purpose as the novel, just as the novel has the same purpose as the drama."[70] The thought of Morrissette, Corrigan, and Greene allows for the real possibility that film novels can be well written and well filmed.

# Notes

## Introduction

1. Madsen, Axel. *John Huston*. Garden City, New York: Doubleday & Company, 1978, 47.
2. Ibid.
3. Ibid., 47–48.
4. Qtd. in Madsen, *John Huston*, 50.
5. Ibid.
6. Wikipedia, "Jack Kerouac," http://en.wikipedia.org/wiki/Jack_kerouac.
7. BYU Magazine, Winter 2002, http://magazine.byu.edu/?act=view &a=847

## Chapter 1

1. The French stage definition of a scene is what happens in one setting at one time with one group of characters. I am using the broader, standard film definition of scene.
2. Qtd. in Hamilton, Ian. *Writers in Hollywood 1915–1951*. London: Heinemann, 1990, 18.
3. Hamilton, *Writers in Hollywood*, 18. For ease of reading, we have added quote marks to the dialogue in the King James Version.
4. Ibid., 19.
5. Alter, Robert. *The Art of Biblical Narrative*. New York: Basic Books, 1981, 63, 82; Bar-Efrat, Shimon. *Narrative Art in the Bible*. Translated by Dorothea Shefer-Vanson and Shimon Bar-Efrat. Sheffield, England: Sheffield Academic Press, l997, 111–21.
6. 2 Kings 5:1.
7. 2 Kings 5:2.
8. 2 Kings 5:3.
9. Spiegel, Alan. *Fiction and the Camera Eye: Visual Consciousness in Film and the Modern Novel*. Charlottesville: University Press of Virginia, 1976, 9–10.
10. Cervantes, Miguel. *The Ingenious Gentleman Don Quixote de la Mancha*. New York: Viking, 1949, 25.
11. Ibid., 26.
12. Ibid., 30.

13. Spiegel, *Fiction and the Camera Eye*, 8.
14. Flaubert, Gustave. *Madame Bovary*. New York: Holt, 1963, 10–11.
15. Ibid., 18.
16. Ibid., 84.
17. Ibid., 11.
18. Ibid., 291–92.
19. Ibid., 291.
20. Ibid., 361.
21. Ibid., 50.
22. Font: Courier 12 pt. Page numbers: upper right. Slugline: left margin 1.5 inches. Acton: left and right margins 1.5 inches. Character name: left margin 4 inches. Dialogue: left and right margins 2.5 inches. Parentheticals: left and right margins 3 inches. Top: .5 inches. Bottom: at least .5 inches. Spacing: double-spaced for everything except paragraphs of action or dialogue.
23. Flaubert, Gustave. *Madame Bovary*, 6.
24. Ibid., 44.
25. Ibid., 362.
26. Ibid., 35.
27. In *Invisible Storytellers* (1988), Kozloff discusses several "Prejudices Against Voice-over Narration," one of which she calls redundancy (8–22). Redundancy occurs when the voice over states something that the picture shows. In defending redundancy, Kozloff explains that "the image of an object and the verbal description of that object exist on two different planes," so that "different information will always be provided by [the] different sign systems" (19–20). But she says that it doesn't work to overlap information when "the action seems banal, the emphasis on it inexplicable" (20). She illustrates this mistake with an insignificant narrated scene from the film *The Old Man and the Sea* (1958). She contrasts that scene with successfully narrated scenes from the film *How Green Was My Valley* (20–21), in which the action is memorable or significant to the narrator.
28. Flaubert, *Madame Bovary*, 111–12.
29. Spiegel, *Fiction and the Camera Eye*, 6.
30. In *A Guide to the Novel* (1965), Richard Eastman writes, "Modern fictional technique is mainly the efflorescence of one conviction: that the novel should be a dramatic rather than assertive art. In the now-hackneyed formula, its rule is: 'Show, don't tell'" (135). This might sound like modern novels don't have a place for narrators, but Eastman explains that they do: modern novelists, he says, first replaced the narrating author with narrating characters, then, more recently, reinstated the narrating author as an "implied author," that is, a fictional one.

31. Spiegel, *Fiction and the Camera Eye*, 6.
32. Ibid., 7.
33. Rayfield, Donald. *Understanding Chekhov: A Critical Study of Chekhov's Prose and Drama*. Wisconsin: University of Wisconsin Press, 1999, 103.
34. Nabokov, Vladimir. *Lectures on Russian Literature*. New York: Harcourt Brace Jovanovich, 1981, 252.
35. Murray, Edward. *The Cinematic Imagination: Writers and the Motion Pictures*. New York: Frederick Ungar Publishing Co., 1972, 124.
36. Ibid., 125; Ellmann, Richard. *James Joyce*. New York: Oxford University Press, 1982, 311.
37. Murray, *The Cinematic Imagination*, 125.
38. Joyce, James. *Ulysses*. New York: Random House, 1986, 3.
39. Ibid., 6.
40. Ibid., 12.
41. Blamires, Harry. *The New Bloomsday Book: A Guide through Ulysses*, 3rd ed. London: Routledge, 1996, 6.
42. Barrow, Craig Wallace. *Montage in James Joyce's Ulysses*. Potomac, Maryland: Studia Humanitas, 1980, 11.
43. Eisenstein, Sergei. *Film Form: Essays in Film Theory*. New York: Meridian Books, 1957, 104.
44. Ibid., 104; Spiegel, *Fiction and the Camera Eye*, 75.
45. Spiegel, *Fiction and the Camera Eye*, 75.
46. Murray, *The Cinematic Imagination*, 4.
47. Ibid., 5.

**Chapter 2**

1. Dreyer, Carl Theodor. *Dreyer in Double Reflection*. New York: E. P. Dutton, 1973, 33.
2. Ibid.
3. Ibid., 33–35.
4. Ibid., 34.
5. Ibid., 34.
6. Ibid., 53.
7. Claude-Edmonde Magny's book—*The Age of the American Novel: The Film Aesthetic of Fiction between the Two Wars*—was published in French in 1948 and in English in 1972.
8. Magny, Claude-Edmonde. *The Age of the American Novel: The Film Aesthetic of Fiction between the Two Wars*. New York: Ungar, 1972, 40–41.
9. Ibid., 44–45.
10. Bazin, André. *What Is Cinema: Volume II*. Los Angeles: University of California Press, 1971, 31.

11. Ibid., 40.
12. Ibid., 39.
13. Ibid., 40.
14. In *Film and Literature: An Introduction* (1979), Morris Beja writes, "Hammett had himself been, like Spade, a private detective in San Francisco (for the Pinkerton Agency) before he began writing his stories and novels, many of which were published in the magazine *Black Mask*" (129).
15. The 1934 Modern Library edition of *The Maltese Falcon* has narration interspersed with scene description on pages 74, 119, 161–62, 182.
16. It is essentially devoid of "interior–subjective" elements—the type of novel Edward Murray would say can't engage readers in understanding characters.
17. Hammett, Dashiell. *The Maltese Falcon*. New York: Modern Library, 1934, 3.
18. Magny, *The Age of the American Novel*, 42–43.
19. Ibid., 41.
20. Ibid., 55–56.
21. Ibid., 41–42.
22. Ibid., 43.
23. Ibid.
24. 43: Magny (*The Age of the American Novel* 1972) contrasts Hammett's hero with the "dull, lifeless, colorless characters who are often interchangeable from one book to another" in "the latest English mysteries"; and with the American–style detectives, "presented as the toughest of tough," though they are most often "nothing but gray policemen who are pale copies of Hammett's Sam Spade (with here and there a light sprinkling of Perry Mason), quite indistinguishable from the criminals they track" (16).
25. Qtd. in Pratley, Gerald. *The Cinema of John Huston*. New York: A. S. Barnes, 1977, 41.
26. Ibid.
27. Ibid., 42.
28. Ibid.
29. Murray, Edward. *The Cinematic Imagination: Writers and the Motion Pictures*. New York: Frederick Ungar Publishing Co., 1972, 157.
30. Ibid., 155.
31. Bloom, Harold, ed. *William Faulkner's Sanctuary*. New York: Chelsea House Publishers, 1988, 27; Spiegel, Alan. *Fiction and the Camera Eye: Visual Consciousness in Film and the Modern Novel*. Charlottesville: University Press of Virginia, 1976, 154.
32. Faulkner, *Sanctuary*, 1.

33. Ibid., 25–26.
34. Magny, *The Age of the American Novel*, 187.
35. Ibid., 188: In l938 and then again in l939, Sartre wrote essays criticizing novels by Faulkner (*Literary* 78–93).
36. Murray, *The Cinematic Imagination*, 162.
37. Magny, *The Age of the American Novel*, 178.
38. Sartre, Jean-Paul. *Literary and Philosophical Essays*. New York: Collier Books, 1955, 78.
39. Ibid.
40. Ibid., 78–79.
41. Ibid., 79.
42. Magny, *The Age of the American Novel*, 181.
43. Bloom, *William Faulkner's Sanctuary*, 14.
44. Murray, *The Cinematic Imagination*, 161–62.
45. Ibid., 161.
46. Qtd. in Millichap, Joseph R. *Steinbeck and Film*. New York: Frederick Ungar Publishing, 1983, 12.
47. Ibid.
48. Ibid.
49. Steinbeck, John. *In Dubious Battle*. New York: Covici-Friede, 1936, 9.
50. Murray, *The Cinematic Imagination*, 265.
51. Steinbeck, John. *Burning Bright: A Play in Story Form*. New York: Viking Press, 1950, 9–13.
52. Magny, *The Age of the American Novel*, 45.
53. Steinbeck, *Sea of Cortez*, 135: Steinbeck's thinking here, and elsewhere, was significantly influenced by the process philosophy of his biologist friend Ed Ricketts. Ricketts chose a quote from Alfred Whitehead's *Science and the Modern World* as the epigraph for one of his famous essays (Astro 47). Whitehead, as I explain in the next chapter, was a leading proponent of process philosophy.
54. Joseph Millichap, in his *Steinbeck and Film*, argues that Steinbeck eventually abandoned the "understanding–acceptance" of his characters. With the advent of World War II, the "objective observation and realistic analysis" of the depression years gave way to "sentimental idealism and patriotic propaganda"(58). Steinbeck, Millichap claims, followed suit with his first novel after *Grapes of Wrath*—*The Moon Is Down*, which presents "melodramatic versions of what totalitarian occupation might be like"(70).
55. Magny, *The Age of the American Novel*, 163.
56. Morrissette, Bruce. *Novel and Film: Essays in Two Genres*. Chicago: University of Chicago Press, 1985, 30.

57. Ibid.
58. Ibid.
59. Sartre, Jean-Paul. *The Chips Are Down*. Boston, Massachusetts: Prime Publishers, 1965, 7–8.
60. Miller, Arthur. *The Misfits*. New York: Viking Press, 1961, ix.
61. Hammen, Scott. *John Huston*. Boston: Twayne, 1985, 97–98.
62. Miller, *The Misfits*, 14–15.
63. Ibid., ix–x.
64. Ibid., x.
65. Ibid., ix.
66. Ibid., 80.
67. Ibid., 2.
68. Ibid., 12.
69. Ibid., 8.
70. Ibid., 13.
71. Madsen, Axel. *John Huston*. Garden City, New York: Doubleday & Company, 1978, 184.
72. Ibid., 183–84.
73. Murray, *The Cinematic Imagination*, 78.
74. Ibid., 79.
75. Morrissette, *Novel and Film*, 33–34.
76. Wolff, Tobias. "Say Yes." *Back in the World*. Boston: Houghton Mifflin, 1985, 57.
77. Phillips, Jayne Anne. "The Heavenly Animal." *American Short Story Masterpieces*, edited by Raymond Carver and Tom Jenks. New York: Delacorte Press 1987, 343.
78. Ibid., 346.

## Chapter 3

1. Sartre, Jean-Paul. *What Is Literature? and Other Essays*. Cambridge: Harvard University Press, 1988, 6.
2. Derrida, Jacques. *Points . . . : Interviews, 1974–1994*. Stanford, California: Stanford University Press, 1995, 345–46.
3. Sartre, Jean-Paul. *Notebooks for an Ethics*. Chicago: University of Chicago Press, 1992, 84.
4. Ibid., 470.
5. Ibid., 522.
6. Sartre, *What Is Literature?* 52–53.
7. Ibid., 48.
8. Ibid., 53.
9. Ibid., 66.

10. Ibid., 50.
11. Ibid., 54.
12. Ibid., 63.
13. Ibid., 65.
14. Ibid., 56.
15. Ibid., 53.
16. Ibid., 55.
17. Ibid., 60.
18. Ibid., 58.
19. Ibid., 54.
20. Ibid., 53.
21. Ibid., 58.
22. Ibid., 63.
23. Ibid., 54.
24. Ibid., 64.
25. Ibid.
26. Ibid., 56.
27. Ibid., 61.
28. Ibid., 66.
29. Derrida, *Points . . . : Interviews*, 347.
30. Sartre, *What Is Literature?* 61.
31. Ibid., 54.
32. Ibid., 65.
33. Ibid., 53.
34. Ibid., 56.
35. Ibid., 67.
36. Derrida, *Points . . . : Interviews*, 350.
37. Sartre, *What Is Literature?* 67.
38. Ibid., 58.
39. Ibid., 67.
40. Rahv, Betty T. *From Sartre to the New Novel.* New York: Kennikat Press, 1974, 6, 11.
41. Ibid., 25.
42. Ibid., 19.
43. Egner, Robert E., and Lester E. Denonn, eds. *The Basic Writings of Bertrand Russell.* New York: Simon and Schuster, 1961, 272.
44. Bar-Efrat, Shimon. *Narrative Art in the Bible.* Translated by Dorothea Shefer-Vanson and Shimon Bar-Efrat. Sheffield, England: Sheffield Academic Press, l997, 90.
45. Moore, Edward C., ed. *Charles S. Peirce: The Essential Writings.* New York: Harper & Row, 1972, 208–9.

46. Ibid., 209.
47. Ibid., 239.
48. Ibid.
49. Ibid., 243.
50. Whitehead, Alfred North. *Adventures of Ideas.* New York: Free Press, 1961, 160.
51. Magny writes that an aesthetic film can be a "synthesizing point of view," a "microcosm" of the universe that produces in others the sense that "everything in the universe, man and things alike, is united in a close solidarity and that each object is connected to all the others in a complete system of reciprocal dependence, from which it derives its own existence." She continues, "This [view] is like the world of simultaneous copresence so well evoked by Jean Wahl (following Whitehead and even Heidegger)—a world in which all objects know one another and in which nothing exists that does not perceive everything else and is not perceived by everything else, as suggested by Bergson in the first and extraordinary chapter of ... *Matter and Memory*" (28). Interestingly enough, these philosophical ideas of connectedness are prominent in the writings of Jean Renoir.
52. Whitehead, *Adventures of Ideas*, 205.
53. Dewey, John. *Ethics: The Middle Works of John Dewey.* Carbondale: Southern Illinois University Press, 1978, 194.
54. 2 Chr 36:13.
55. Prov 21:29.
56. Prov 15:1.
57. Prov 25:15.
58. Meredith, George, and Henri, Bergson. *Comedy: An Essay on Comedy and Laughter.* Baltimore: John Hopkins University Press, 1956, 179–80.
59. Aristotle. *Aristotle Poetics.* Translated by Gerald F. Else. Ann Arbor: University of Michigan Press, 1967, 23.

### Chapter 4

1. Aristotle. *Aristotle Poetics.* Translated by Gerald F. Else. Ann Arbor: University of Michigan Press, 1967, 47.
2. Heidegger, Martin. *The Fundamental Concepts of Metaphysics: World, Finitude, Solitude.* Bloomington: Indiana University Press, 1995, 343.
3. Ibid., 342–43.
4. Aristotle, *Aristotle Poetics*, 47.
5. Aristotle, *Aristotle Poetics*, 43.

## Chapter 5

1. Leitch, Thomas M. *What Stories Are: Narrative Theory and Interpretation.* University Park, Pennsylvania: Pennsylvania State University Press, 1986, 72.
2. Moore, Edward C., ed. *Charles S. Peirce: The Essential Writings.* New York: Harper & Row, 1972, 209.
3. McKee, Robert. *Story.* New York: HarperEntertainment, 1997, 138.
4. Bazin, André. *What Is Cinema: Volume II.* Los Angeles: University of California Press, 1971, 60.
5. McKee, *Story*, 190.
6. Aristotle. *Aristotle Poetics.* Translated by Gerald F. Else. Ann Arbor: University of Michigan Press, 1967, 30.
7. Ibid., 49–50.
8. Johnston, Sibyl. Readings: English 5K and 5L. Unpublished, 1998, 10.
9. Ibid.
10. Ibid., 73.
11. Heidegger, Martin. *Parmenides.* Bloomington: Indiana University Press, 1992, 85.
12. Heidegger, Martin. *Basic Writings.* New York: HarperSanFrancisco, 1993, 186–87.
13. Qtd. in Johnston, *Where the Stories Come From*, 190.
14. Johnston, Sibyl. *Where the Stories Come From: Beginning to Write Fiction.* New York: Longman, 2002, 66.
15. Oida, Yoshi, and Lorna Marshall. *The Invisible Actor.* London: Methuen, 1997, 109.
16. Ibid., 86.

## Chapter 6

1. Green, Henry. Surviving: The Uncollected Writings of Henry Green. New York: Viking, 1992, 143–50.
2. Seger, Linda. Making a Good Script Great. New York: Dodd, Mead, & Company, 1987, 40–42.
3. Bar-Efrat, Shimon. Narrative Art in the Bible. Translated by Dorothea Shefer-Vanson and Shimon Bar-Efrat. Sheffield, England: Sheffield Academic Press, 1997, 169.
4. Ibid., 103–5.
5. http://www.the-leaky-cauldron.org/2006/11/13/transcript-of-em-order-of-the-phoenix-em-teaser-trailer

## Chapter 7

1. Renoir, Jean. *Renoir on Renoir: Interviews, Essays, and Remarks.* Cambridge: Cambridge University Press, 1989, 82.
2. Johnston, Sibyl. *Where the Stories Come From: Beginning to Write Fiction.* New York: Longman, 2002, 179.
3. Leitch, Thomas M. *What Stories Are: Narrative Theory and Interpretation.* University Park, Pennsylvania: Pennsylvania State University Press, 1986, 38.
4. McKee, Robert. *Story.* New York: HarperEntertainment, 1997, 344.
5. Johnston, Sibyl. Readings: English 5K and 5L. Unpublished, 1998, 19.
6. Ibid., 56–57.
7. Ibid., 57.
8. Ibid., 95.

## Chapter 8

1. Johnston, Sibyl. *The Longman Guide to Writing Beginning Fiction.* New York: Pearson Longman, 2007, 104.
2. Berlin, Adele. *Poetics and Interpretation of Biblical Narrative.* Sheffield, England: Almond Press, 1983, 70.
3. Johnston, Sibyl. Readings: English 5K and 5L. Unpublished, 1998, 19.
4. Johnston, Sibyl. *Where the Stories Come From: Beginning to Write Fiction.* New York: Longman, 2002, 100.
5. Ibid., 24.
6. Ibid., 97.
7. Ibid., 105.
8. Stern, Jerome, *Making Shapely Fiction.* New York: W. W. Norton & Company, 1991, 245–46.
9. Ibid., 129.
10. Gardner, John, *The Art of Fiction.* New York: Knopf, 1984, 111.

## Chapter 9

1. Renoir, Jean. *My Life and My Films.* New York: Atheneum, 1974, 156.
2. Renoir, Jean. *Renoir on Renoir: Interviews, Essays, and Remarks.* Cambridge: Cambridge University Press, 1989, 154.
3. Katz, Steven D. *Film Directing Shot by Shot.* Stoneham, Massachussets: Focal Press:, 1991, 267.
4. See Jerome T. Walsh's *Style & Structure in Biblical Hebrew Narrative.* Collegeville, Minnesota: Liturgical Press, 2001.

5. Wikipedia, "Jafar Panahi," http://en.wikipedia.org/wiki/Jafar_Panahi.
6. Stanislavski, Constantin, *An Actor Prepares*. New York: Routledge/Theatre Arts Books, 1964, 85.
7. Benedetti, Jean. *Stanislavski & the Actor*. Great Britain: Methuen Drama, 1998, 106.
8. In *Renoir on Renoir,* p. 249, Renoir speaks similarly about getting something strongly in mind and then "forgetting" it in the moment: I'm very influenced by and become very engrossed in actors, and so I try to have a subject firmly in mind before I start, because once I start, I forget it. I think of only one thing: how to express the personality of the actor within the framework of a defined role.
9. Stanislavski, *An Actor Prepares*, 193.
10. See note 8.

## The possibility of film novels

1. Bluestone, George. *Novels into Film*. Baltimore: Johns Hopkins Press, 1957, 5.
2. Ibid., vi.
3. Whether a novel *should* be transferred directly to film—because the two media themselves are sufficiently different—or should *not* be transferred directly to film—because a film should always add a significant difference to a story to merit a change in medium—are interesting and valid questions. But these aren't the questions I deal with in this survey. My concern here is whether a novel *can* be transferred to film and whether a good novel can be transferred into a good film.
4. Bluestone, *Novels into Film, 63.
5. Ibid., 117.
6. Ibid., 118.
7. Ibid., 119.
8. Ibid., 117–18.
9. Ibid., 120.
10. Ibid., 121.
11. Ibid.
12. Ibid., 122.
13. Ibid., 211.
14. Ib*id.*, 47.
15. Murray, Edward. *The Cinematic Imagination: Writers and the Motion Pictures*. New York: Frederick Ungar Publishing Co., 1972, 78, 143, 147, 205, 214, 295.
16. Ibid., 263.

17. Ibid., 264.
18. These essays were first published in French in the late 1960s and early 1970s.
19. The term alludes to Einstein's unsuccessful search, during the last 30 years of his life, for a "unified field theory" which would unite general relativity (his own theory of space-time and gravitation) with Maxwell's theory of electromagnetism.
20. Morrissette, Bruce. *Novel and Film: Essays in Two Genres.* Chicago: University of Chicago Press, 1985, 28.
21. Ibid., 38.
22. Ibid., 25.
23. Ibid., 27.
24. Ibid., 15.
25. Ibid., 25.
26. Ibid., 26.
27. Ibid., 12.
28. Ibid., 15.
29. Ibid., 17.
30. Ibid., 21.
31. Ibid., 27.
32. Ibid., 20–21, 27.
33. Ibid., 70.
34. Ibid., 28.
35. Ibid., 29.
36. Ibid.
37. Ibid.
38. Ibid., 30.
39. Ibid., 29.
40. Ibid., 13.
41. Ibid., 33.
42. Ibid.
43. Corrigan, Timothy. *Film and Literature: An Introduction and Reader.* New Jersey: Prentice Hall, 1999, 1–2.
44. Ibid., 22.
45. Ibid., 29.
46. Ibid., 42.
47. Ibid., 57.
48. Ibid., 60–61.
49. Ibid., 71.
50. Ibid., 71.
51. Ibid., 37, 93.

52. Ibid., 60.
53. Ibid., 61.
54. Morrissette, *Novel and Film*, 29.
55. Ibid., 58.
56. Bluestone, *Novels into Film*, 218.
57. Murray, *The Cinematic Imagination*, 295.
58. Qtd. in Murray, *The Cinematic Imagination*, 143.
59. Ibid., 143–44.
60. Murray, *The Cinematic Imagination*, 291. In the first half of his book, Murray argues that "film scenarios in the guise of plays"(102) don't make for good plays. In the second half, he argues, with parallel reasoning, that film scenarios in the guise of fiction(291) don't make for good novels. He cites Steinbeck as an example of an author who wrote film scenarios as fiction and in doing so "confused novel writing with scenario writing"(275), which amounted to "an evasion of his obligations as a serious artist"(277).
61. Murray 134, 157, 243. This viewpoint is repeated, without support, by Brian McFarlane: "However persuasively it may be demonstrated that the likes of Joyce, Faulkner, and Hemingway have drawn on cinematic techniques, the fact is that the cinema has been more at home with novels from—or descended from—an earlier period"(6).
62. Murray, *The Cinematic Imagination*, 128.
63. Ibid., 134.
64. Ibid.
65. Ibid., 102.
66. Ibid., 273.
67. Ibid., 296.
68. Murray does recognize that he hasn't written a poetics, but "instructive lessons" for a future "poetics of adaptation" (*The Cinematic Imagination*, 67).
69. Morrissette, *Novel and Film*, 39.
70. Qtd. in Beja, Morris. *Film and Literature: An Introduction*. New York: Longman, 1979, 51.

# Bibliography

Alter, Robert. *The Art of Biblical Narrative*. New York: Basic Books, 1981.

Aristotle. *Aristotle Poetics*. Translated by Gerald F. Else. Ann Arbor: University of Michigan Press, 1967.

Astro, Richard. *John Steinbeck and Edward F. Ricketts: the Shaping of a Novelist*. Minneapolis: University of Minnesota Press, 1973.

Bar-Efrat, Shimon. *Narrative Art in the Bible*. Translated by Dorothea Shefer-Vanson and Shimon Bar-Efrat. Sheffield, England: Sheffield Academic Press, l997.

Barrow, Craig Wallace. *Montage in James Joyce's Ulysses*. Potomac, Maryland: Studia Humanitas, 1980.

Bazin, André. *What Is Cinema: Volume II*. Los Angeles: University of California Press, 1971.

Beja, Morris. *Film and Literature: An Introduction*. New York: Longman, 1979.

Benedetti, Jean. *Stanislavski & the Actor*. London: Methuen, 1998.

Berlin, Adele. *Poetics and Interpretation of Biblical Narrative*. Sheffield, England: Almond Press, 1983.

Blamires, Harry. *The New Bloomsday Book: A Guide through Ulysses*, 3rd ed. London: Routledge, 1996.

Bloom, Harold, ed. *William Faulkner's Sanctuary*. New York: Chelsea House Publishers, 1988.

Bluestone, George. *Novels into Film*. Baltimore: Johns Hopkins Press, 1957.

Cervantes, Miguel. *The Ingenious Gentleman Don Quixote de la Mancha*. New York: Viking, 1949.

Corrigan, Timothy. *Film and Literature: An Introduction and Reader*. New Jersey: Prentice Hall, 1999.

Derrida, Jacques. *Points ... : Interviews, 1974–1994*. Stanford, California: Stanford University Press, 1995.

Dewey, John. *Ethics: The Middle Works of John Dewey*. Carbondale: Southern Illinois University Press, 1978.

Dreyer, Carl Theodor. *Dreyer in Double Reflection*. New York: E. P. Dutton, 1973.

Dreyer, Carl Theodor. *Four Screenplays*. Bloomington: Indiana University Press, 1970.

Eastman, Richard M. *A Guide to the Novel*. San Francisco: Chandler, 1965.

Egner, Robert E., and Lester E. Denonn, eds. *The Basic Writings of Bertrand Russell*. New York: Simon and Schuster, 1961.

Eisenstein, Sergei. *Film Form: Essays in Film Theory*. New York: Meridian Books, 1957.

Elbow, Peter. *Writing with Power: Techniques for Mastering the Writing Process*. New York: Oxford University Press, 1981.

Ellmann, Richard. *James Joyce*. New York: Oxford University Press, 1982.

Faulkner, William. *Sanctuary*. New York: Modern Library, 1932.

Flaubert, Gustave. *Madame Bovary*. New York: Holt, 1963.

Gardner, John, *The Art of Fiction*. New York: Knopf, 1984.

Green, Henry. *Loving* (1945). New York: Penguin, 1978.

Green, Henry. *Surviving: The Uncollected Writings of Henry Green*. New York: Viking, 1992.

Hamilton, Ian. *Writers in Hollywood 1915–1951*. London: Heinemann, 1990.

Hammen, Scott. *John Huston*. Boston: Twayne, 1985.

Hammett, Dashiell. *The Maltese Falcon*. New York: Modern Library, 1934.

Heidegger, Martin. *Basic Writings*. New York: HarperSanFrancisco, 1993.

Heidegger, Martin. *The Fundamental Concepts of Metaphysics: World, Finitude, Solitude*. Bloomington: Indiana University Press, 1995.

Heidegger, Martin. *Parmenides*. Bloomington: Indiana University Press, 1992.

Johnston, Sibyl. Readings: English 5K and 5L. Unpublished, 1998.

Johnston, Sibyl. *Where the Stories Come From: Beginning to Write Fiction*. New York: Longman, 2002.

Johnston, Sibyl. *The Longman Guide to Writing Beginning Fiction*. New York: Pearson Longman, 2007.

Joyce, James. *Ulysses*. New York: Random House, 1986.

Katz, Steven D. *Film Directing Shot by Shot*. Stoneham, Massachusetts: Focal Press, 1991.

Kozloff, Sarah. *Invisible Storytellers: Voice-Over Narration in American Fiction Film*. Berkeley: University of California Press, 1988.

Leitch, Thomas M. *What Stories Are: Narrative Theory and Interpretation*. University Park, Pennsylvania: Pennsylvania State University Press, 1986.

McFarlane, Brian. *Novel to Film: An Introduction to the Theory of Adaptation*. Oxford: Clarendon, 1996.

McKee, Robert. *Story*. New York: HarperEntertainment, 1997.

Madsen, Axel. *John Huston*. Garden City, New York: Doubleday & Company, 1978.

Magny, Claude-Edmonde. *The Age of the American Novel: The Film Aesthetic of Fiction between the Two Wars*. New York: Ungar, 1972.

Meredith, George, and Henri Bergson. *Comedy: An Essay on Comedy* and *Laughter*. Baltimore: Johns Hopkins University Press, 1956.

Miller, Arthur. *The Misfits*. New York: Viking Press, 1961.

Millichap, Joseph R. *Steinbeck and Film*. New York: Frederick Ungar Publishing, 1983.

Moore, Edward C., ed. *Charles S. Peirce: The Essential Writings*. New York: Harper & Row, 1972.

Morrissette, Bruce. *Novel and Film: Essays in Two Genres*. Chicago: University of Chicago Press, 1985.

Murray, Edward. *The Cinematic Imagination: Writers and the Motion Pictures*. New York: Frederick Ungar Publishing Co., 1972.

Nabokov, Vladimir. *Lectures on Russian Literature*. New York: Harcourt Brace Jovanovich, 1981.

Oida, Yoshi, and Lorna Marshall. *The Invisible Actor*. London: Methuen, 1997.

Phillips, Jayne Anne. "The Heavenly Animal." *American Short Story Masterpieces*, edited by Raymond Carver and Tom Jenks. New York: Delacorte Press 1987, 340–52.

Pratley, Gerald. *The Cinema of John Huston*. New York: A. S. Barnes, 1977.

Pudovkin, V. "Film Acting: Two Phases." *Acting: A Handbook of the Stanislavski Method*. New York: Crown, 1955.

Rahv, Betty T. *From Sartre to the New Novel*. New York: Kennikat Press, 1974.

Rayfield, Donald. *Understanding Chekhov: A Critical Study of Chekhov's Prose and Drama*. Madison, Wisconsin: University of Wisconsin Press, 1999.

Renoir, Jean. *My Life and My Films*. New York: Atheneum, 1974.

Renoir, Jean. *Renoir on Renoir: Interviews, Essays, and Remarks*. Cambridge: Cambridge University Press, 1989.

Sartre, Jean-Paul. *The Chips Are Down*. Boston, Massachusetts: Prime Publishers, 1965.

Sartre, Jean-Paul. *Literary and Philosophical Essays*. New York: Collier Books, 1955.

Sartre, Jean-Paul. *Notebooks for an Ethics*. Chicago: University of Chicago Press, 1992.

Sartre, Jean-Paul. *What Is Literature? and Other Essays*. Cambridge: Harvard University Press, 1988.

Seger, Linda. *Making a Good Script Great*. New York: Dodd, Mead, & Company, 1987.

Spiegel, Alan. *Fiction and the Camera Eye: Visual Consciousness in Film and the Modern Novel*. Charlottesville: University Press of Virginia, 1976.

Stanislavski, Constantin. *An Actor Prepares*. New York: Routledge/Theatre Arts Books, 1964.

Stanislavski, Constantin. *Creating a Role*. New York: Routledge/Theatre Arts Books, 1961.

Starkie, Enid. *Flaubert: The Making of the Master*. New York: Atheneum, 1967.

Steinbeck, John. *Burning Bright: A Play in Story Form.* New York: Viking Press, 1950.

Steinbeck, John. *In Dubious Battle.* New York: Covici-Friede, 1936.

Steinbeck, John. *Of Mice and Men.* New York: Penguin Books, 1993.

Steinbeck, John. *The Log from the Sea of Cortez.* New York: Viking Press, 1951.

Stern, Jerome, *Making Shapely Fiction.* New York: W. W. Norton & Company, 1991.

Walsh, Jerome T. *Style & Structure in Biblical Hebrew Narrative.* Collegeville, Minnesota: Liturgical Press, 2001.

Whitehead, Alfred North. *Adventures of Ideas.* New York: Free Press, 1961.

Wolff, Tobias. "Say Yes." *Back in the World.* Boston: Houghton Mifflin, 1985, 55–62.

Zola, Émile. *The Works of Emile Zola.* New York: Walter J. Black, 1928.

# Index

Page numbers in **bold** denote figures/photographs.